ROBERT YATES RACING

BEN WHITE

MBI Publishing Company

Dedication

There are many people who have played such a large part in this story. I dedicate this book to them. Those people are my parents, J. Clyde and V. C Yates; my brothers and sisters, Sarah Goare, Rachel Wall, John Clyde Yates Jr., Martha Brady, Phyllis Goff, Elaine Rogers, Doris Rogers, and Richard Yates. I also dedicate this to my wife, Carolyn Yates, our son, Doug Yates, and our daughter, Amy Yates Davy.

Finally, I would like to acknowledge some special people I worked with in racing over the years. They are John Holman, Ralph Moody, Junior Johnson, Bill Gardner, the late Jim Gardner, and the late Harry Ranier. A very special thank you goes out to each one of you.

—*Robert Yates*

As the author of this book, I dedicate this work to several very special people who have since departed this earth for eternal life in heaven. Those people are Mrs. Henrietta W. White, Davey Allison, Adam Petty, Kenny Irwin, Tony Roper, and Dale Earnhardt. I will always cherish the gifts each one of you gave to me. The most special gift of all was the honor of being in your presence.

—*Ben White*

First published in 2001 by MBI Publishing Company, Galtier Plaza, Suite 200, 380 Jackson Street, St. Paul, MN 55101-3885 USA

© White, Ben. 2001

MBI Publishing Company books are also available at discounts in bulk quantity for industrial or sales-promotional use. For details write to Special Sales Manager at Motorbooks International Wholesalers & Distributors, Galtier Plaza, Suite 200, 380 Jackson Street, St. Paul, MN 55101-3885 USA.

Library of Congress Cataloging-in-Publication Data Available
ISBN: 0-7603-0865-9

Edited by Amy Glaser
Designed by Jim Snyder

Printed in China

On the front cover: Dale Jarrett. Robert Yates. Davey Allison. The No. 88 UPS car. All four are legends in NASCAR. *Nigel Kinrade photo*

On the frontispiece: Amid Jarrett's red driving shoes are million-dollar reminders of his great day at Talladega in 1998. *Nigel Kinrade photo*

On the title page: Jarrett leads the field at Talladega, where he eventually finished 18th on the leap lap due to being held back in the draft. *Nigel Kinrade photo*

On the back cover: Jarrett celebrating a win at Talladega in 1998. The 28 and 88 cars at Charlotte in 1999. Robert Yates. *Nigel Kinrade photo*

Author Bio: Ben White has previously written books on NASCAR racing for MBI Publishing. White is a well-known authority on NASCAR and is an editor for *Winston Cup Illustrated* magazine. White, his wife Eva, and son Aaron live in Salisbury, North Carolina.

Contents

Acknowledgments **6**

Introduction **7**

Chapter **ONE**   *The **Early Years*** **11**

Chapter **TWO**   ***Engines** and **Horsepower*** **25**

Chapter **THREE**   ***Joining Ranier Racing** and **Choosing Davey Allison*** . **45**

Chapter **FOUR**   ***Ernie Irvan*** **81**

Chapter **FIVE**   ***Kenny Irwin*** **103**

Chapter **SIX**   ***Dale Jarrett Joins Robert Yates Racing*** **113**

Chapter **SEVEN**   ***Ricky Rudd*** **143**

Epilogue **152**

Index **155**

Acknowledgments

Over the course of time, the fascinating story of Robert Yates and the Yates family has slowly come together on these pages for one and all to enjoy. There are many people I would like to thank for their contributions to this project. First and foremost, I thank Robert Yates for so graciously giving me his time on a number of occasions to talk about the good times and the emotional, personal struggles, as well as all of those wonderfully enlightening stories that make him such a special individual. Thank you Carolyn Yates, Doug Yates, and Amy Yates Davy for your support of this book through quotes as well as family information and rare personal photos. Your generosity and support of this project is most appreciated.

Weekend after weekend I met Robert at the race tracks of the Winston Cup circuit and we found a quiet place to talk. Robert often found time away from both of his championship-caliber teams to reminisce about the past. I sincerely thank you for your faith in me to write this book and for giving me so much of your time, even when you really didn't have it to spare. You have been very generous and kind and I will always appreciate our friendship.

Thank you also Richard Yates for your tremendous help in reconstructing stories, searching for photos, and generally helping put this book together. You have been a great friend and I really appreciate that gift.

Thank you Dale Jarrett, Ricky Rudd, and Ernie Irvan for giving your time and offering your perspectives on your present tenures with Robert, as well as your expressions of admiration for Robert himself. I really appreciate the long-standing friendships I've shared with you all over nearly 20 years of Winston Cup racing.

A special thank you is extended to Lee Klancher of MBI Publishing Company for having tremendous patience while these pages were being written. I extend a sincere thank you to Amy Glaser for her tremendous editing talents. There were many road blocks, but your kindness and understanding under some difficult circumstances paved the way for this project to become a success. I will forever be grateful to you both. Thanks also to Joseph Cabadas for your editing help. Special thanks goes to Whitney Shaw of Street and Smith's Sports Group for allowing me to use information from *NASCAR Winston Cup Scene* and *NASCAR Winston Cup Illustrated* for reference, as well as various quotes used from those publications. They have been most helpful.

Also, thanks to colleagues Steve Waid, Jeff Owens, Deb Williams, Art Weinstein, Kenny Bruce, Rick Houston, and Mark Ashenfelter for your support and advice. Your sharing of personal experiences with Robert over the years was very helpful in my efforts to present him and his family more clearly.

I would like to express a special thank you to my wife, Eva, and son, Aaron, for your continued support for yet another book project. Thank you to my father, Ben N. White Jr.; brothers Cullen and Doug White; my sisters Phyllis Jones, Becky Brown, and Shelly Sapp; and aunt and uncle, Edna Ruth and Blair Trewhitt, for your continued support and encouragement concerning every book I write. Thanks also goes out to Libby Gant and Julie Larson. Thank you to photographers David Chobat, Cindy Karam Elliott, Jim Fluharty, David Gemmill, Don Hunter, Elmer Kappel, Nigel Kinrade, and Tim Wilcox. Their beautiful photography has joined the words of this book to make the story come to life. Finally, I would like to thank the readers for choosing this book for a visit with Robert Yates and the Yates family. Each chapter and photo is presented for your enjoyment.

—Ben White

Introduction

Looking at the man and his intense interest in the automobile and its speed, it's difficult to associate any endeavor other than racing with Robert Yates. When Yates was introduced to the fledgling NASCAR Winston Cup (then known as Grand National) circuit in 1962, he was a young man desperately searching for his place in this world. He found his place as a successful, highly respected fixture in NASCAR.

When Yates was a teenager, fast cars and drag races on the streets of Charlotte, North Carolina, were a huge part of his life, a part that often got him in trouble with the local police and his highly respected parents.

In the early 1960s, Yates saw his first NASCAR race. At the time, drivers such as Junior Johnson, Fireball Roberts, and Fred Lorenzen were the stars making the headlines.

Yates soon graduated from the streets to local short track racing and Grand National racing, which seemed to satisfy the competitive fire inside of him. He could drive cars fast, and NASCAR stock car racing was a natural proving ground where aggressiveness was transformed into horsepower.

Several decades have passed since those early, searching years. And if someone had told the young Yates that he would become one of the most famous engine builders and team owners in NASCAR's 53-year history, he would have been unable to comprehend the prophesy of such a statement.

Nonetheless, he was in heaven in 1967 when he began his engine builder's position at Holman-Moody, Ford's stellar factory operation—a position he'd applied for on a whim. The hours were long and often spanned from early morning to late at night, but Yates did not perceive that as a negative. He had no concept of time when he worked to transform bored blocks of metal into some of the most powerful pole-position-winning engines on the circuit.

After Holman–Moody, Yates went on to work for Junior Johnson and Digard Racing. He would eventually buy the team from his boss, Harry Ranier; and that's when things would begin to fall into place. Davey Allison, driver for Ranier's team, was the one who encouraged Yates to buy the team. Allison knew the potential that was within Robert Yates.

Some of the best known drivers in the sport turned steering wheels for Yates and helped build a once financially struggling operation into one of the most powerful teams NASCAR has known since its official formation in 1948. Allison, Lake Speed, Ernie Irvan, Kenny Wallace, Robby Gordon, Dale Jarrett, Kenny Irwin, and Ricky Rudd have all found success in Yates' Fords. They read as a "Who's Who" list of famous names in auto racing. Most of the Yates team's success came from the No. 28 and No. 88 vehicles, cars that placed them in the record books for all time.

"Without a doubt, had Davey Allison not given me the confidence I needed to buy this race team, there is no telling where I would be today," Yates says. "Davey kept telling me, 'You can do this! You can do this! You don't need a partner! You can become a successful team owner!'

"Since he [Davey] said those words back in 1988, so much has happened with these race teams. Davey saw the future during those days when a decision had to be made. He knew in his heart we could win races and championships. We've won a lot of races in both the No. 28 and No. 88 and the Winston Cup championship in 1999 with Dale Jarrett. . . .

"I'm grateful to Davey and all of the drivers who have made this organization a success", Yates continues. "It's their talent and the talent of so many people who have worked hard behind the scenes that has made this all possible. Because of their accomplishments, we have quite a story to tell."

CHAPTER ONE

The *Early Years*

Robert Yates was born to speed. Born with a need to stand out among his eight siblings, even his twin brother and closest confidant, Richard. He was a daredevil at heart.

"Robert had a lot of willpower and would not give up on anything that got in his head," Richard says. "He was a daredevil. If you dared him to jump off a building, he would do it. He would jump off the garage roof into the leaves . . . thinking he was Superman. It didn't matter what it was. If it was in a car, Robert was going to bet you he could outrun you. That was just Robert."

The war games that the twin brothers played in the summer of 1950 in Charlotte, North Carolina, illustrate Robert's bold spirit, and its propensity for placing him in physical danger.

In an alleyway nicknamed "the Plaza," two towheaded boys dodged and weaved as they fired BB guns at each other, using trashcan lids as shields. The two young Yates boys had escaped the watchful eyes of their mother and seemed oblivious to their game's peril, while the sounds of small copper balls ringing off metal filled the alley.

"Yes, we did shoot each other with BB guns as kids," Robert says. "The trick was to use the trashcan lids to keep from getting stung in the face with them. It's a wonder we didn't lose an eye. We probably worried our poor mother every day. We took some chances from time to time."

Similar hair-raising incidents made the "Dennis the Menace" cartoon character in the newspapers seem tame when compared with Robert and Richard Yates. Yet, the twin brothers were best friends and did everything together, Robert recalls.

Robert and Richard entertained themselves well during their formative years, but what was seemingly normal for other families didn't always apply at the Yates residence. They were the sons of the pastor of the Allen Street Baptist Church, and as such, didn't live a life of privilege, but they made the best of what they had.

"We didn't have any money, but we would always come up with things to play with," Robert says. "We really didn't seem to want for anything."

"We had a lot of fun when we were children," Richard remembers. "When we were growing up, we didn't have a television at all, so we didn't know who movie stars or TV stars were. When we were 16 years old, we didn't know who John Wayne was."

Instead of watching TV, the two boys built huts and fortresses and dug tunnels around their yard and played war games with neighborhood kids there and in the Plaza behind their house. They built a clubhouse in the back yard that had a trap door so the kids could climb out into a clump of trees. And the yard had a fishpond where goldfish swam. The back yard "was downtown as far as being a real sharp place to hang out," Robert recalls. "We had a ball growing up."

The Yates boys also enjoyed gentle pleasures such as flying kites and making walkie-talkies out of orange juice cans—before engaging in their next dangerous endeavor.

Fortunately for the two mischievous boys, their Mom was always there, Robert remembers. "I couldn't imagine what kind of child I would have been had our mother not been there. I would have been in a lot of trouble. . . . Usually, it was Mom who was there to patch up cuts or keep us healing up so we would be in good enough shape to go out and get hurt again."

Robert (left) and Richard sit quietly at only a few months of age in this photo taken in the summer 1943 at their home in Charlotte.
Richard Yates collection

On August 21, 1948, Richard (front) and Robert (back) enjoy a pony ride in front of their house on Allen Street in Charlotte, North Carolina. *Richard Yates collection*

A Mother's Touch

Robert and Richard Yates were the youngest of nine children of one of the city's most well-known families, which was headed by the Reverend John Clyde Yates and his wife, V. C. Cook Yates.

Mrs. Yates was a woman who stood firm, physically and from a disciplinary angle. Born in Amity Hill, North Carolina, the name on her birth certificate was "V. C." No one but her parents really knew what the initials stood for. Some said the letters stood for "Virginia Carolina," but she often joked that it meant "Very Cute."

Coming from a large farm, V. C. knew nothing but hard work and long hours, many spent making her family's clothes. With shoulders hunched slightly and eyes struggling to see the tiny marks of her patterns, she would sit at the sewing machine for hours, mending or creating the dresses for her daughters and pants and shirts for her sons. Every shirt Robert wore until the 11th grade was carefully handmade by his mother.

Other priorities for Mrs. Yates included supporting her church and seeking an education for her children. While growing up, she was at the top of her class. She was determined that her children also would learn. But Robert, her youngest son, always felt he failed her with his homework; he had other interests.

Richard readily agreed with his brother that there were simply too many other adventures to be explored and going to Midwood Elementary School, a block away from their house, cut deeply into their plans.

"We struggled a little bit with that because we didn't like to do homework," Richard says. "The rest of our brothers and sisters were straight-A students. We did good in school, but still didn't like school much.

"Being the youngest of nine children, I don't think our parents could control me and Robert very much. We were pretty rambunctious. If mother would have a bad day with us she would tell (Daddy) and get him riled up enough that he would get a hickory switch after us. We didn't get it too many times, but we knew right from wrong."

Of the two parents, however, it was usually Mrs. Yates who broke the hickory switches from backyard bushes when needed to settle domestic disputes among members of the brood. She made sure the family was in top working order.

Pillar of the Community

The Rev. John Yates, a native of Statesville, North Carolina, was highly respected by everyone who heard him. A graduate of Wake Forest

Robert (left) poses with his young family and sister in May 1971. Standing in front of Robert is his son Doug, and wife Carolyn is holding daughter Amy. Robert's sister Martha Yates Brady, is on the right.

Seminary in Wake Forest, North Carolina, he enjoyed reading and studied a vast assortment of topics from his personal collection of about 6,000 books.

The one object that seemed out of place in his study was a 20-to-30-pound iron bar. The Rev. Yates used it like a barbell in order to keep his physical stamina as strong as his ministerial spirit.

"Dad was a big man," Robert says with reverence. "He was 6 feet 2 inches, but he probably looked 10 feet tall to me. He really had to do the workouts because he would have to have strength enough to hold men and women when he baptized them. He wanted them to stand at attention and sort of put them back into the water, but to do that he had to be strong. So if a man was 350 pounds and asked to be baptized, then [Dad] simply had to be strong enough to hold him and not drop him." The Rev. Yates lifted that bar for so many years that he left an imprint of his hands at both ends, Robert adds.

The Rev. Yates acted as easy and calm as the love of the God he so adamantly and faithfully studied. But when need be, his voice rang out from the pulpit on Sunday and echoed off the church walls.

"He was extremely patient and quiet," Robert says. "He very seldom raised his voice for any reason. When he got up in the pulpit he never stuttered or lost his place in his sermons. He usually had no notes. He would do the entire sermon from memory."

Robert said that his father loved to tell jokes to the family, but otherwise, he listened more than he talked. So, when The Reverend did talk, people listened, especially his children.

From a very early age, Robert said that he looked at his dad in awe. There were rules to follow and little or no negotiations were allowed.

Home Sweet Home

The Yates children were Sarah, Rachael, John Clyde Jr., Martha, Phyllis, Elaine, Doris, Richard, and finally Robert. Richard had beaten his brother into the world by 19 minutes.

The first house that Richard and Robert remember was a white frame house—like an old mill house—that had a front room, a kitchen, a bathroom, and a couple of bedrooms.

"There was also a long hallway at the back of the house and that's where me and Robert had our baby cribs," Richard said. "That same house was heated by coal and I remember me and Robert would go down to where the coal, was and just sit there and play in it. What a mess that was.

In 1949, the Yates children stand out front of their home at The Plaza. From left to right are: friend Sue Swann, Elaine Yates, and Doris Yates. Standing in front are Richard and Robert Yates, who were six years old at the time. *Courtesy of Elaine Yates Rogers*

"Robert also liked to play with matches and he set the house on fire one day. They got it out before the house burned down but our mother about had a stroke over that. Robert was about five years old at the time."

As was customary for preachers, the Allen Street house was just a few feet from the front doors of the Allen Street Baptist Church, but it was torn down to add space to the church. So, the Yates family moved to a nearby, large, old brick house that was located on a street with a wide median between the lanes.

"The house was one of the nicest in Charlotte at the time, and it belonged to the church. It was a big brick house with a big slate roof, big columns, and a big front porch. It was located only a few blocks from the church (on Allen Street) and is still standing today. On occasions, I'll find myself going by there and I always look over to see it as I pass by," Robert says.

A Safe Haven

No matter where the Yates lived, the dining room table was often filled with bowls and platters of steaming hot food that smelled delicious. Meals were a rare time when the entire Yates family gathered, with everyone coming in from different directions.

Quite often, V. C. Yates and her daughters cooked the meals, but it was The Rev. John Yates' job to make breakfast. Robert and Richard remember hearing the sizzle and smelling the aroma of ham and eggs as they came down the stairway from their rooms upstairs.

A Yates' staple was corn mush, which is similar to Southern grits but more like corn meal in consistency. It was less expensive than grits and very good with red-eye gravy.

"We loved fried chicken and creamed potatoes, virtually anything you could imagine," Robert remembers. "We ate really good. People who were members of the church would all the time bring us vegetables. We had a lot of meals brought to the house."

Laughter filled the house, too, as did the sound of music coming from the Yates family's various instruments. Often the family kept the lights burning well after established Saturday night bedtimes. Robert says that he loved hearing his older siblings play the piano and, for a time, he even tried his hands on its keys.

The result of those late-night music sessions was that the Yates boys needed to suppress yawns during their father's Sunday morning sermons. But, there was the day when music caused Robert to sing a very unhappy tune.

Cuts and Concussions

"There was a time when we had a neighbor who was a train engineer," Robert says. "We would be out playing between his house and our house and he liked us.

"Anyway, he gave each of us a little harmonica. My family was pretty much a musical family, except me and Richard. We played these harmonicas and either I lost mine or Richard lost his. I'd say the other one was mine and he would say it was his, but there were no names on them. We would find one and then claim it to be ours and fight over it."

During one of their disputes over the harmonica, Richard chased his twin brother through the living room and into the music room. "There were French doors and the door knobs were glass and I used the glass door knob to make a turn to the den. I ripped my hand on that door knob, and it was bleeding really bad," Robert says.

That was just one of any number of scuffles and wrestling matches that the twin boys had both inside their home and outside. Aggressive drives sometimes overrode Robert and Richard's better judgment, and hostilities were occasionally acted out in dramatic and dangerous ways.

"We had a chinaberry tree in the back yard and we liked to climb," Richard says. "There was a rock garden below it and I pushed Robert out of that tree one day." Robert fell into the rock garden's fishpond, hitting his head on the rocks, and was knocked out. "He had a skull fracture out of the deal, so anytime he goes off the deep end we figure that's the reason," Richard says.

"I was knocked out four times as a child because of stuff like that," Robert adds. "I was also shoved through a window and got knocked out when I fell through the glass and dropped about 12 feet into the basement."

Another boyhood tussle left young Robert bleeding profusely when a wayward knife found its way much too close to a main artery in his hand.

Robert recalls that he was hitting his brother with a coat hanger when Richard responded by stabbing him once in the wrist with the pointed razor blade of an Exacto knife. The blood from the wound spurted 3 feet into the air. Luckily, one of Robert's sisters, Elaine, knew to put her hand over the cut, apply pressure, and march her wayward brother to the doctor's office three blocks from their home.

"I probably would have bled to death had she not been there. I was probably six or seven years old at the time," Robert says. "I still have the scar from it."

Robert and Richard Yates enjoy a new train set in 1957 at age 14. *Courtesy of Elaine Yates Rogers*

The Yates family gather at the 10th anniversary of their father's, Rev. J. Clyde Yates, tenure as minister of Allen Street Baptist Church in this 1953 photo. Ten-year-old Robert is in the front row at left, and Richard is on the right. *Courtesy of Elaine Yates Rogers*

Perfect Behavior

The Yates twins' rougher tendencies stood in stark contrast to their behavior in church. There, anything less than ideal behavior was simply unacceptable. Sitting on a long, hard wooden bench under their father's stare, the boys did not even think of crossing the line to discover the consequences of an offense.

"Things like chewing gum and writing notes and cutting up wasn't tolerated. When you went into the church, you were respectful. The atmosphere was formal. There wasn't a lot of jabbering or talking. But it wasn't one of those deals where a baby would be dismissed for crying out," Robert says.

There were only a couple of times on Sunday evening when the Rev. John Yates had to stop preaching to chastise someone. "I was always just so glad it wasn't my row he was calling down," Robert adds.

The Rev. Yates spent many long days looking after the concerns of his parishioners, the sick in the city's hospital, and those confined to home. He led prayers during a crisis, presided over countless weddings and funerals, and even

drove people to the store for groceries. There was always something that required his personal touch and so many were thankful for it. Both Robert and Richard, and sometimes the entire family, accompanied the Rev. Yates to various sites when time permitted.

"I remember the first car we had was a 1937 Chevrolet," Robert says. "All 11 of us could get in it and drive up to Ridgecrest, which was a Baptist camp near Asheville, North Carolina. Me and Richard would stand up, and the car had enough room where you could put orange crates in the back so everyone would have a seat. Those trips to Ridgecrest were all-day trips, but we had a lot of fun doing them."

One stop on the way was a favorite, Robert says. "I remember one of our church members had a Gulf service station. We would always go and watch the guys who worked there service the cars that came in. They would change the oil and grease the cars and change spark plugs and service the battery. I was just fascinated by all that was going on. I just paid attention to everything they were doing," Robert recalls.

His fascination with cars, especially working on their components, began to grow.

Paying to Play

Robert Yates and his twin brother began tinkering with old lawn mower engines, pulling them off their frames and then mounting them in hand-built go-carts made out of two-by-fours. To find out how fast they would go, they would sneak off to an open space and open them up at full speed.

Their hobby wasn't cheap, however. They needed to buy fuel and parts for the go-cart, so they went to work, collecting and selling papers for the Chesapeake Paper Company in Charlotte and cutting lawns.

"The advantage we had was the fact our dad was a pastor, so we knew everybody. The church members would save their papers and Dad would drive the car and we would pick up. The church congregation would call on us to mow their grass because we were well known in the community," Richard says.

At 14 or 15 years of age, the Yates brothers began delivering the *Charlotte News* and later the *Charlotte Observer* in order to make money. "That meant you'd get up at four in the morning and deliver papers and then go to school. So it was a rigorous schedule. You had to keep it up everyday because people depended on having their newspapers on the porch every morning," Richard said.

In addition to their paper routes, Robert and Richard began washing cars, keeping the loose change they found under the seats and in between the cushions. Robert and Richard saved their money and had their sights set on a bicycle. Like any young boys, bicycles were a big part of their early teenage years.

"I just couldn't wait until we had cut enough grass to afford a bike," Robert recalls. But, one of the church members decided to give them a spare bicycle. "I think we cut the grass and maybe gave them $12 for it. It was blue and white with fenders and whitewall tires," Robert says.

Robert and Richard shared the bicycle, but they were rough on it. The chain would fall off and then they'd lose the wheel bearings, so they had to learn how to fix it. "We would break the brake system on it and would have to get that fixed. We learned how to work on bicycles just from the need to fix them," Robert says.

Fast Times, Fast Cars

As he entered junior and then senior high school, Robert wanted to play sports, but his parents were worried about his health. When he was younger, Robert had rheumatic fever, which left him with a heart murmur. "The doctors and my parents didn't want me to do a lot of strenuous exercise," Robert says. "I wanted to play sports and my mom wouldn't let me because I had this heart problem. I could play church ball, but I couldn't play junior high ball. That ticked me off."

Unable to pursue his love of sports, Robert turned his energies toward working on cars. "Instead of being on the field in the afternoons, I was at home working on go-carts," he says. "We had a double-car garage there on the Plaza and it had a dirt floor, but it was a nice dirt floor. It was hard and you could roll a creeper around on

it because it was smooth. My dad had a few tools. He would let me use them to take bicycles and go-carts apart."

As Robert and Richard became teenagers in the spring of 1957, there were many new challenges and experiences ahead of them. In the meantime, Buddy Baker, an occasional participant at the goings on at the Plaza and member of Allen Street Baptist Church, became a more central figure in young Robert Yates' life and, no doubt, helped foster his desire for speed.

Buddy Baker was the son of two-time NASCAR Winston Cup (then called Grand National) champion Buck Baker. Plus, the young

Richard Yates, friend Ralph Faulk, and Robert Yates stop their bicycles long enough for a photograph to be taken at their home on The Plaza in 1958 when the boys were 16 years old. *Courtesy of Elaine Yates Rogers*

On December 30, 1960, Elaine Yates was married to Jerry Rogers at the Eastway Baptist Church in Charlotte, N.C. From left to right are: Don Rogers, Richard Yates, Doris Yates, Clyde Yates Jr., Elaine Yates Rogers, Rev. J.C. Yates Sr., Jerry Rogers, Steve Rogers, Phyllis Rollins, Robert Yates, Ava Gosnell, and Larry Rogers. *Courtesy of Elaine Yates Rogers*

Baker would grow up to win 20 Winston Cup races himself, including three victories at the 600-mile races held at what is now Lowe's Motor Speedway in nearby Concord, North Carolina.

Buddy Baker is now one of NASCAR's most loved broadcasters and is known for his huge laugh and comical storytelling. Even when he was growing up, Baker kept the crowd laughing.

"I met Robert at the church and thought 'what a nice, calm little guy.' I lived on Barry Street and the Yates family lived on 'the Plaza.' Although we lived less than five blocks from each other, we didn't hang out together all the time, but he was a friend," Baker recalls.

Robert Yates went to Bible study sessions, worked with the youth of the church, and ushered during church services, just as a preacher's son would do, Baker said. But he added that young Robert's interests fell elsewhere.

"Then I really got to know him. I found later he was a loose cannon. He liked all the things young guys like, like fast cars and working on cars," Baker says.

Buddy's house was a magnet for kids who liked cars. Late at night, one could walk by and find the light burning in Baker's garage as the sounds of race engines broke the silence of the neighborhood streets. "My father had a race

This rare family photo taken in the early shows the entire Yates family. Back row from left to right are John Clyde Jr., Richard, John Clyde Sr., and Robert. Second row, left to right are Phyllis, Rachel, Sarah, Martha, V. C., Elaine, and Doris. *Richard Yates collection*

shop that was pretty centrally located between the Allen Street church and my house. Kids would come up there and hang out and I'm sure Robert was there many times," Buddy remembers. "The race shop then was kind of like a garage that worked on street cars, too. We had three employees and that was it, but it was an exciting place to be, both for a guy who wanted to drive race cars, and another guy, Robert, who was excited about working on them."

Robert remembers how Baker kept inviting him to join him at races. Robert often thought of his parents and what their reaction to such a venture might be. "He kept asking me to go to a race with him. I said, 'My dad would kill me if I did that.' I had a lot of respect for my parents and I didn't see anything wrong with racing, but I wouldn't go against my parents," Robert says.

But, like many a teenage boy, Robert and Richard Yates began obsessing about owning a car of their own. No doubt, seeing the activity at Buddy Baker's house fueled their desire,

even though neither Yates twin knew what the National Association for Stock Car Auto Racing was about.

Every Boy's Dream

Robert and Richard's dream was to own a car. To accomplish that goal, they kept delivering papers and served hamburgers and French fries to hungry customers at restaurants.

The Rev. John Yates saw how his sons worked all hours of the day and night in various jobs to make money. So, despite the fact that Robert and Richard were too young to get a North Carolina driver's license, he gave his twin sons a black 1947 Pontiac. The old car had been a gift to the Rev. Yates from a member of his congregation. The car was bent, a result of its first owner running into a horse, but the front-end damage had been fixed and the car repainted.

That old Pontiac set the foundation of Robert's reputation for building some of the strongest engines in stock-car racing. He would

During their parents 50th wedding anniversary on June 27, 1971, all but one of the children were present for the special day. From left to right are Robert, Elaine, Richard, Phyllis, Doris, Sarah, Clyde, Jr., and Rachel. Sister Martha was not present.
Courtesy of Elaine Yates Rogers

soon learn, without a doubt, that he was a true shade-tree mechanic and that he had racing in his blood.

A True Calling

"We worked on our car together, paid for it together, shared it, and when we tore it up racing, we had to fix it," Robert says, recalling the Pontiac. "So we learned how to be good mechanics. We went out and paid cash for it. That was our first vehicle and we went on to build engines and race cars."

The Pontiac didn't last long, however. The Yates brothers traded it in and, with the $1,700 they had saved, bought a new 1957 Chevrolet. That '57 Chevy was a huge investment for the two boys.

Then, in the fashion of those who raced stock cars, the boys boldly modified the car so that it would run faster on Charlotte's side streets. "Over the years, we had seven different engines in the car, everything from fuel injection to six two-barreled carburetors to two four-barrels," Robert remembers. "We had every kind of transmission and rear end in it. We knew that car forward and backward. Every single function of a '57 Chevrolet—we could about fix it blindfolded."

By Robert's 16th birthday on April 19, 1959, he had already had plenty of experience behind the wheel of various cars. The fact that he didn't technically have a license to operate a vehicle certainly wasn't going to keep him from testing the modifications he had just finished making.

Of course, not everything was fun and games; Robert had to continue working hard to support his growing passion for cars.

Burning the Midnight Oil

"I worked at Babe Malloy's restaurant for several years when I was in high school," Robert says. "It was a drive-in restaurant and there were two locations. One was in Asheville and the other in Charlotte. I did everything from working the curb and taking orders to pretty much running the place. I've peeled a lot of potatoes, fried a lot of chicken, and made a lot of sandwiches."

He worked at night, going to bed around midnight; but then he had to get up by 3:30 A.M. to deliver papers. Robert says that he always felt sleepy and had poor grades in school. He wasn't a social climber—didn't go to parties—because he worked every night.

"It wasn't like I didn't know anybody or was unsociable. I just worked. You might say I was a workaholic to support myself, but I enjoyed work. Working on cars was fun. I would have done it probably without getting paid any money. The fact I enjoyed it and got paid to do it was a treat," Robert says.

There was only one thing that kept him working all the crazy hours: cars and how badly he wanted to work on them and drive them.

Owning the Streets

Long before Yates even knew about NASCAR, building engines and tinkering under hoods was his natural obsession. Buddy Baker recalls the patient, fine-tuned modifications on Robert's car in high school. "I remember if there was a sharp car sitting outside the high school, it was his [Robert's]. It had to have the latest of everything on it. He certainly wasn't from a rich family, but he managed," Baker says.

When school ended for the day, Robert and Baker would hop into their cars and terrorize the streets. "We did run around together, and I had a 1957 Chevrolet and he also had one," Baker says. "I was going to be a race car driver and he was going to do what he wanted to do, but he turned out to be one of the greatest engine builders in the history of the NASCAR."

Both boys were competitive, and Robert says that he outran Buddy once while drag racing in the street, but Baker disagrees with Yates' tale, which seems to grow more dramatic with each passing year.

"He [Robert] keeps telling the story about how he outran me in a street car. Well, I admit

I've been hit on the head a few times, but I don't remember that one," Baker says.

In 1957, Robert was finally old enough to have a driver's license, which was the prize for a boy who sat in school daydreaming about what he would do to the car that night. Unfortunately, he wasn't able to keep his license.

Trouble as a Teenager

Robert's right foot could be blamed for a lot of the problems he suffered in high school. His inability to keep the gas pedal off the floor caused a lot of friction with the Charlotte police department, and just as much trouble with his parents. More than one evening was spent in his father's study explaining his latest speeding ticket or run-in with other high school kids with fast equipment to challenge him.

To make matters worse, Robert was floundering in school. The bottom line was that he had to find his place in life.

Robert's parents, John Clyde Yates Sr, (left) and V. C. Cooke Yates, pose at their 50th wedding anniversary celebration, held at the Allen Street Baptist Church in 1971. *Richard Yates collection*

21

"When you get to that age where you look at being a mechanic as not being a real job, you say to yourself, 'What am I going to do? I don't want to be a preacher,'" Robert says. "My dad always pushed education. He wouldn't give me money for a Coca-Cola, but he would buy me any book I wanted or any textbook I needed. He would push education and that's what I would rebel against. I didn't have good grades. I didn't want to go to school. I didn't want to embarrass [my parents] by dropping out."

Mr. and Mrs. Yates had to do something to help get their son's life in order or the young risk taker would most certainly end up in jail. So, they took Robert's license away after he received one too many speeding tickets for trying to outrun the Charlotte police. This action, Robert admits, was the best thing to happen at that point in his life because he got his life back on track.

In 1959, Robert started racing at Shuffletown (North Carolina) Dragway, located on the outskirts of Charlotte. He kept it a secret from parents and family, but those he told were at least thankful he wasn't doing it on the city's streets, but still, Robert's risk-taking behind the wheel had to be moderated before he hurt himself or someone else.

Rescue Plan

Robert's sister Martha and her husband, Otis Brady, were studying at the Wake Forest Seminary in Wake Forest, North Carolina. They realized that Robert had to leave home in order to find his own way and settle down. So, they came up with a plan.

"My sister asked me to come and live with them for a year, go to school, and get something going for myself. They were real nice the way they put it, but they basically told me I was a nut or an idiot behind the wheel," Robert remembers.

Robert reluctantly agreed to his sister's idea and moved to Wake Forest. He had to make a number of adjustments, including making new friends, and it was certainly difficult at times, but Martha's patience with Robert paid off.

"The first three months of that just about killed me. I didn't have a license, so I couldn't drive a car. That meant I had to walk just about everywhere," Robert says. "I loved cars and to have to walk away from them really killed me."

Robert made a dramatic change in his priorities, though. In the summer of 1961 he graduated from Wake Forest High School as a straight-A student. It had been a complete turnaround, but the need for speed was still in his blood.

Robert's Introduction to NASCAR

In February of 1959, Bill France Sr., who had founded NASCAR 11 years earlier, had just put the finishing touches on his other creation—the Daytona International Speedway, located in Daytona Beach, Florida.

Where drivers once raced on the actual sands of the beach, a 2.5-mile superspeedway now stood. The mouths of drivers and mechanics dropped in awe when they first saw it. Other than the Indianapolis Motor Speedway or Darlington (South Carolina) track, there wasn't anything like Daytona.

"In 1963, me and a bunch of guys from school loaded up and went down to Daytona," Robert remembers. "As far as the track goes, I had never seen anything that big in my life. It was quite a place to see for the first time, and like everybody else, I thought the place was huge.

"After we got to the track, we walked down to the fence. They were having a Sportsmans race that day and we were standing there when they had an 11-car pile-up. One of the windshields went crashing down between us. That was a pretty scary deal, but watching them race around the place was pretty exciting."

Pursuing his mechanical inclinations, Yates went to Wilson Technical College in Wilson, North Carolina and graduated in 1964 with a degree in mechanical engineering. Then, for a few months, he took various technical classes at Mars Hill College, but didn't graduate.

Robert had found a small race track within walking distance of Mars Hill. With his license still suspended from his earlier highway endeavors, he had no choice but to enjoy the walk.

As fate would have it, he met his first motorsports hero at Asheville-Weaverville (North Carolina) Speedway where he used to walk from Mars Hill. Yates recalls seeing Junior Johnson at the race. Johnson wore a pair of overalls and a white T-shirt, not the uniforms that race car drivers would later wear. "Since [Junior Johnson] was the first guy I saw, I pulled for him in the race. He put on a heck of a show and won the race. I still remember that day like it was yesterday," Robert says.

As the sun began to set over the trees at the end of the day, Robert Yates walked home, thinking about the thrilling race. Still, he had no way of knowing his life would later take a very unexpected turn that would put him right in the center of it all.

Junior Johnson wheels his famed No. 3 Chevrolet down the backstretch at Daytona International Speedway in February 1963. This photo was taken the day Robert witnessed his first NASCAR Winston Cup (then Grand National) race. *Don Hunter photo*

CHAPTER **TWO**

Engines and *Horsepower*

Robert was right at home pounding metal amid the smell of grease lingering in the air. And that's just what he was doing in the spring of 1967—except that he was not working on race cars; instead he was repairing tractor engines. Still, it did deal with the mechanical workings of a machine, and Robert had no complaints. Mechanical chores were something he'd become quite accustomed to, and something he'd enjoyed since his days of building makeshift go-carts on the Plaza with Richard.

Robert refurbished big pieces of machinery at Western Carolina Tractor Company in Charlotte. They were an International Harvester dealer in the area and conducted business in several states. Robert had a keen ability for assembling and disassembling various mechanical jobs with great speed and accuracy. It was a job he truly enjoyed.

"I covered the deal," Yates says. "The foreman really moved me around and gave me a good opportunity. If I was good at doing something, he would stick me on it. I did (bulldozer) tracks, old stuff, and rebuilt various things. We had a great foreman who wanted me to learn a lot. I wasn't one to stay on something long and massage a deal out.

"There were guys there whining that would say, 'I want to do this, I don't want to do that. I want to work on the new stuff.' I tell kids today how they should do the very best they can with what they are asked to do. I got some good opportunities because I didn't whine about it. I would knock out the dirtiest, nastiest job, and then the next one would be nice."

Robert found his niche on the power-shift transmission, an automatic transmission. It's a particular piece of equipment he soon found himself servicing for all branches of the company. "There were four branches—Asheville, Columbia, Charlotte, and Greenville—and they would ship them [power-shift transmissions] in from other branches for me to work on because I didn't have a comeback about not wanting to work on them."

Listening to Another Man's Dream

Every day like clockwork, one co-worker would walk up and begin his usual daily declaration to anyone within earshot who would listen. "Hey, Robert, when it comes to NASCAR, you know that Fords are the only things that matter on a race track. You know that, right?" the co-worker asked with a degree of authority in his voice. "You know what it means, right? Ford means, 'First on Race Day!'"

"Yeah, sure," Robert would say, sort of looking up from his manual. "Whatever you say. First on race day!"

"Well, guess what else?" the co-worker asked. "I'm here to tell you I'm going to get a job down there at Holman-Moody building race cars for a living! Working on these ol' bulldozers is hard work, but boy, wouldn't that be heaven—turning wrenches on a Ford and making it win on Sunday! You just watch. I'm going to be a H-M employee real soon. You just wait and see. Just like they say, their engines are 'Competition Proven.'"

In this 1962 photo of the inside of the Holman-Moody shop, Ford passenger cars are being converted to NASCAR stock cars. *Don Hunter photo*

25

"Yeah, that's what they say, alright," Robert returned. "'Competition Proven!'"

"I've put in an application and I've been calling them, you know, to check on things. Holman-Moody is the place to be. At least it will be for me, anyway." The co-worker rambled on, but Robert wasn't interested.

Holman-Moody was a factory for building race cars to be shipped to anyone with enough cash to buy one. The organization was Ford's racing arm, with a $30 million annual budget and a large number of employees. They were the number one race car suppliers of the time. The other auto makers didn't have an operation that would even compare to Holman-Moody.

The race cars produced were turnkey and painted to one's desire. For $30,000 one could buy a Holman-Moody race car, a truck, and a few extra parts to become a full-fledged race car driver. Back in 1968, $30,000 was quite a bit of money, but it was still in an affordable price range. Few race cars were sold to the general public, though. A race car driver had to have good financial backing and, of course, skill to drive the high-banked speedways.

At the height of their existence, Holman-Moody had a division of top-name drivers wheeling their cars on the NASCAR circuit each week. The idea was to show they could win on the race track, which would help promote sales of race cars to those wanting to race as regulars on the circuit.

Through the years, drivers such as Glenn "Fireball" Roberts, Fred Lorenzen, Dick Hutherson, Ned Jarrett, Bobby Allison, and Mario Andretti had all taken Holman-Moody Fords to victory lane. David Pearson won the 1968 NASCAR Grand National championship, as well as the 1969 season long title in an H-M car.

Although, NASCAR racing was fun to watch and read about, Robert had other responsibilities to worry about. He never really considered working for Holman-Moody. His mind was still quite devoted to the jobs that needed to be completed at his full-time job.

Each morning and afternoon, Robert tackled some pretty tough jobs at the tractor company involving huge gears, tracks, pistons, and drivetrains. Each morning and afternoon, the co-worker simply talked Robert to near death about stock-car racing, Holman-Moody, and Ford. Robert agreed wholeheartedly that a Ford was a great car, but he didn't want to talk about them every minute of the day.

"A guy I worked with there at Western Carolina Tractor Company was just a fanatic about Fords," Robert remembers. "He would talk about Fords day and night, and he would talk about Holman-Moody to the point where I didn't want to know any more about Holman-Moody. He knew everything about the place. He would just bug them to death about getting a job over there, but before that time, I had never even thought about making a living through racing. It had never crossed my mind."

Then, to Robert's surprise, Jim Brown, a friend who was employed at Holman-Moody, called Robert with a request. "I got a call one day from Jim Brown asking if I would be interested in a job at Holman-Moody working on engines," Robert remembers. "Like I said, I hadn't even given the idea any thought, but the friend (Brown) told me it was pretty much a done deal if I wanted a job. The money was better, with a lot of overtime hours available, which meant the money would be better than the normal rate of pay promised."

What attracted Holman-Moody to Yates was his stellar ability to build engines quickly with great precision. Holman-Moody's operation was conducted in assembly-line fashion, just like auto makers' building passenger cars in Detroit. Brown knew Robert would fit the bill perfectly.

After some serious discussions with Carolyn, his wife, Robert took the job. From the moment the two had met a few years earlier as teenagers in Charlotte, Carolyn had always been a supporter of Robert's dreams and goals. Robert and Carolyn were married on September 7, 1965. The two were still very early into their marriage and any financial security they could gain would be nothing but an advantage. Robert was now a father to Doug, who was not even a year old at the time. To turn the job down might very well be a mistake. Robert soon informed his supervisor at Western

One of the most famous Fords ever to roll out of Holman-Moody was the white No. 28 Galaxie driven by Fred Lorenzen. Ralph Moody and John Holman are standing alongside their famous race car. *Don Hunter photo*

The two men behind the powerhouse Holman-Moody Ford operation were Ralph Moody (left) and John Holman. *Don Hunter*

Holman-Moody, and after that episode, the tractor company didn't want him, either.

Robert had been making $2.25 an hour at Western Carolina Tractor, and that was about as much as he would ever make there. A fellow employee had been with the company more than 30 years and made only $2.50 an hour. The job at Holman-Moody paid $4.00 an hour, but within 24 hours, Jack "Sully" Sullivan, Yates' supervisor and crew chief for driver Fred Lorenzen, said, "Hey, by the way, we're not going to pay you $4.00 an hour." Robert was surprised, thinking for a second he may have made a mistake. "Instead, we're going to pay you $4.50. You don't have a problem with that, do you?" Robert smiled and was relieved it would be more than he was told instead of less.

The money coming into the Yates' checking account was the most they had seen since being married. The price for that security was that Robert had to put in an average of 100 hours a week, seven days a week. The ace engine builder and mechanic didn't mind the job at all, as it was something he truly enjoyed. Another added benefit was the fact that there were no grease-covered jobs that needed his attention in the hot summer sun or cold of winter. At Holman-Moody, one could literally see his or her reflection in the shiny waxed floors. Work stations were kept spotless, and the tools and equipment were treated like surgical tools. The employee list was over 325, and each person wore crisp, white work shirts and pants as if they were hospital workers. Like Robert's former co-worker had imagined, working at Holman-Moody was like working in Ford heaven.

There was a downside to the luxurious surroundings and well-equipped work environment, though. Some employees were convinced that John Holman was the devil in disguise. To work for Holman meant total loyalty and perfection every time out. It also meant total tolerance for his angry temper, which exploded at the blink of an eye. Men lost their jobs for the smallest of infractions. Robert remembers witnessing one such intolerant incident at the parts counter, where a worker stood waiting for an order to be filled. While there, the worker

Carolina Tractor Company of his intentions to take the job, and well wishes were given.

The co-worker who so badly wanted to work at Holman-Moody didn't take the news of Robert's employment there too lightly. In a fit of bitterness and rage, the young man hopped aboard a large bulldozer that needed to be serviced and proceeded to run through some of the building's garage doors. Obviously, he had more problems than not being selected at

Ralph Moody and John Holman look over a new Ford engine that has just been built for one of the many stock cars set to roll out of the Charlotte, North Carolina, facility. *Don Hunter photo*

rested his elbows on the counter top, only for a few seconds. Around the corner came Holman, who went for the man like a hungry shark craving meat.

"What do you think you're doing?" shouted Holman to the rattled employee.

"I'm standing here, sir, just waiting for parts," he finally muttered.

"Well, while you're standing there waiting for your parts, you stand at attention! Do you understand what I'm saying to you? You stand any other way and you'll be out of here standing on the street."

"Yes sir," the worker said, as if being belittled by a military drill sergeant.

Holman would find someone a step out of place and chew them out in front of groups of people to set an example.

"John Holman was a guy that everyone at Holman-Moody absolutely feared," Robert remembers. "He paid you well and he expected you to be hard at work at your work station. If he came by and you weren't turning a wrench

of some kind, he would scream. He was there waiting for the next victim to chew out."

In most cases, those unpredictable quakes came because Holman had either been reamed by some Ford executive in Detroit or possibly had a disagreement with Ralph Moody, the other partner in Holman-Moody and a driver-turned-mechanical wizard. Moody could find that needed chassis tweak or engine boost that helped make the careers of many drivers. To be noticed by Moody was like money in the bank. He was an early-day Ray Evernham, a man who was ultra-smart and successful on and off the track. In the late 1950s through the late 1960s, he was "the man" when it came to stock-car racing.

Unfortunately, through many years of operating the Holman-Moody enterprise, the two principal parties had more than one loud discussion over something to do with the business. Their relationship had the ups and downs of a roller coaster and the turbulence of a 747, and those within shouting distance usually were

29

Bobby Allison takes to the high banks of Michigan Speedway in July 1972. That season, he won 10 races and finished second to Richard Petty in the season-long points battle.
Don Hunter Photo

swept up in their wake. Very early one morning, Robert encountered Holman and was certain his job had been lost.

"It was about three o'clock in the morning and I was building connecting rods, changing caps, doing some grinding for engines, and I've got three machines running," Robert remembers. "Here comes Holman around the corner screaming about oil out in the aisle that I had let run over.

"He saw me, stopped, and went from that angry look to saying, 'Hey, I'm sorry.' I was shaking. A few minutes pass and this guy starts telling me his life story. We talked for a long time. I remember him telling me that night, 'I wasn't born a son of a bitch. Life has just made me one.'"

Accepting Robert's Role in Racing

Robert's parents were quite strict with him and his brothers and sisters while growing up in Charlotte. He wondered how his mother would take to the fact that he was working with race cars on Sundays. Not surprisingly, V. C. was upset about Robert working on the Sabbath day, and she thought car racing was a sinful career.

"I probably told them I was doing engine development, which I was," Robert says. "Once I got involved in a team, she would say things like, 'You're there at the race track and you're there with a race team.' She didn't want me to be associated in any way with racers. She thought they were undesirable people. She didn't like to call me in and preach to me, but she loved and worried about her son. She never came and told me 'I don't want you doing that.' I think she had a lot of wishful thinking, wishing I wouldn't [get into the car racing sport]. It sort of went against the grain of what they had worked so hard to accomplish; trying to get people out of dance halls and pool halls, places where people tend to go bad.

"The only time she entered a race track was at Charlotte in 1973. We had a teardown of this big engine deal. She, my daughter Amy, and Carolyn were trying to find me. They came to the race track and tried to break through the

Junior Johnson cleans the windshield of Cale Yarborough's Chevrolet at Darlington in 1973. *Don Hunter photo*

guards to find me. She [Robert's mother] never saw a race at a race track, but she did see a few on television."

Robert was working with Holman-Moody in 1970 when Ford's motorsports arm was seeing its darkest days. In essence, the campaign to get as many Fords on the race track as possible had been successful; so much so that the majority of the cars being used were Fords, which limited the number of spots available for competition against the Ford products by Chrysler, Pontiac, or Chevrolet.

Chrysler's effort went to the Pettys and team owner Cotton Owens, and team owner Nord Kraskopf and reigning champion Bobby Isaac. Chevrolet had not had the factory support of its cars since 1963. Ford was so prominent on the race track it virtually had nothing against which to compete.

The work force at Holman-Moody had grown to 325 employees, but 25 to 30 employees per week were given pink slips. There weren't enough orders to fill and not enough work to justify such a huge staff. Yates, however, felt a bit optimistic. Holman took a keen liking to Yates for his ability to work on an engine with accurate precision at lightning speed.

"I really felt we had a great relationship together," Yates says of Holman. "A lot of people absolutely did not want to be around Holman for any reason for fear they would be raked over the coals just for breathing. To my surprise, our relationship was almost a father-son kind of a deal."

Holman came to Robert's workstation one day and asked if he would like to attend a school to learn turbine engines. Robert said he would like to attend, and Holman informed him it was an all-expense paid course and would be no charge to him.

Little time passed before Holman issued free reign to Robert in the company's parts room. Those parts often ended up on a short track race car Robert had been tinkering with. Robert had a job with Holman for as long as he wanted it. With the economic times as rough as they were, he may have been working on Holman's own Lincoln Continental, but Robert would have a job.

One afternoon in 1970, Robert received a call from Bill Allman. Bill is the brother of Bud Allman, the engine builder who had worked on cars for team owner Junior Johnson. Johnson, the moonshiner-turned-racer, had partnered with Charlotte Motor Speedway president Richard Howard and started a race team. Howard was the team owner while Johnson had a share of the team and acted as crew chief.

Howard and Johnson were working to get Chevrolet back in the fold, and they had hoped tickets could be sold on the Chevrolet angle. Johnson was looking for that hidden magic he knew existed within the Monte Carlo Chevrolet since it had been designed with a long nose and hood area. The Monte Carlo would serve as one of the best weight-distributed cars on the track, and without a doubt, make an excellent race car for both the superspeedways and short tracks. There was only one flaw with the Chevrolet Monte Carlo, and that was the engine. Very few mechanics had worked on the engine that was provided for it, and few could make it successfully hold up for the 600 grueling miles of the event at Charlotte Motor Speedway. It had been years since Johnson had pushed the throttles of the 1963 Chevrolet engines, and they were simply foreign to many regulars in the garage area. Johnson knew of only one man who could make them win again: Robert Yates.

In his conversation with Robert, Bud Allman referred to the Chevrolet engines he had unpacked at Johnson's shop as "school bus" engines and refused to work on them. With the Holman-Moody situation becoming rather shaky, and Robert anxious about his future, Robert

Charlie Glotzbach goes through the fourth turn at Charlotte in the 1971 World 600. *Don Hunter photo*

Charlie Glotzbach is all smiles with his trophy in hand after one of his four wins. *Don Hunter photo*

33

Junior Johnson stands alongside Linda Vaughn after winning the 1963 National 400 at Charlotte. He would be a large part of Robert Yates' life less than a decade later. *Don Hunter photo*

agreed to drive from Charlotte to North Wilkesboro to see what Allman had uncovered.

"I was just going up to Junior's to look at what they had and see if they [the engines] could be made race ready," Robert says. "I looked it over and felt it had some potential, but me and Junior never once talked about money because at the time, Junior didn't have any and Richard Howard had put about all he could into building the car. There just wasn't any money to be had."

Robert punched the clock at Holman-Moody, talked with John Holman from time to time, and drove to North Wilkesboro after work each night to get Junior's engines running. That meant absolutely no time at home with Carolyn or the children.

"I would get off work at 6:00 or 6:30 P.M., grab a hot dog to eat on the way, get to Junior's, and start working again," Robert

remembers. "I would work on those engines until 3:00 or 4:00 in the morning, sleep a few hours, and then go to work for Holman-Moody. I got four engines ready to put in the race car over a couple of months time. I did all this just to try and help Junior."

Little did anyone know Robert was building the Ford engines being campaigned by Holman-Moody driver Bobby Allison, as well as the Chevrolet engine in Howard's Chevrolet that was driven by Charlie Glotzbach. Holman would have exploded if he had known that the little white Chevrolet Johnson was fielding to beat his Fords had a Robert Yates engine under its hood.

"I was afraid I was going to get fired," Yates says. "I was standing in the infield at Charlotte Motor Speedway cheering for the little white Chevrolet to kick everybody's butt and still work for Holman. I don't know why

This battle in the 1971 World 600 was especially exciting to Robert Yates. Unknown to the majority of the racing world, Yates built the engine in the Holman-Moody No. 12 Mercury driven by Bobby Allison, as well as the No. 3 Chevrolet that was owned by Richard Howard and driven by Charlie Glotzbach. Allison won the race, and Glotzbach crashed and finished 28th. *Don Hunter photo*

Bobby Allison pulls his Holman-Moody Ford into the fueling area at Lowe's Motor Speedway (then Charlotte Motor Speedway) in 1971. *David Gemmill photo*

In this photograph, circa 1960s, Robert tightens bolts on one of the countless engines he built while at Holman-Moody.
Don Hunter photo

he didn't fire me, but I really thought Ford needed some competition.

"On the clock, I was Holman's. Off the clock, I did my own thing. I guess that's how he looked at it. Plus, I think Holman knew the Ford factory racing operation was about over."

Finally, Robert ended his employment with Holman-Moody even though there were more projects to be completed, many of which were outside of racing. Robert could no longer work for free and still pay his bills. He decided to operate a filling station with longtime friend Horace "Smitty" Smith in the Charlotte area. Smith also helped work on Johnson's race cars and was a good friend to Robert.

One afternoon while working at Johnson's shop, Smitty complained of a tingling feeling in his arms. On his way home that night, Smitty suffered a heart attack and died in a car crash near his Norwood, North Carolina, home.

After Smitty's funeral, Johnson paid Yates for all of his hard work and support during the months he worked to get the race team started. Johnson gave Yates a $100 bill and a 427 race engine to sell for cash. Junior Johnson said, "Robert is one of those great engine builders who could get a lot from his motors. He came to our team because so many people talked about what a great engine builder he was, and still is today. He helped us win a lot of races with his motors."

In August 1971, Robert officially joined Johnson's team as a full time team member. The commute back and forth from Charlotte was long, and Johnson offered Robert a house he owned in North Wilkesboro. On New Year's Day 1971, the family packed and moved to the country. Doug Yates remembers those early days of living close to Johnson's shop and growing up around race cars.

"My dad was always working night and day to get to where he is. He was always on winning teams and that's what made me proud of him. It seemed like everywhere he went they won or had a chance to win. I could sense even from an early age that good things were happening to him with the team he worked for winning as much as they did.

Cale Yarborough drives Junior Johnson's Chevrolet through a turn at Darlington (South Carolina) Raceway with a Robert Yates engine on board. *Don Hunter photo*

Yarborough is all smiles after another great run. The majority of his 83 career wins came with help from Robert Yates engines. *Don Hunter photo*

In the mid-1970s, Yates turned wrenches on engines at the famed Digard Racing Company operation that was owned by Bill and Jim Gardner. From left to right in this engine room photo are Buddy Parrott, Ducky Newman, Jim Gardner, Yates, and James Harper. *Don Hunter photo*

"I remember when I was a little boy about five or six years old, I would be at Junior Johnson's shop and he would be working late and he had a cot there," Doug says. "I would sit on that cot and watch him [Robert] work or I would sit on the floor and sort nuts and bolts and hang out with him while he worked all night."

Doug recalls the time when his family lived on a farm in the country while his father was working for Junior Johnson. "It was a real small house. You could walk to the shop. The house had a basement and that is where we had go-carts and motorcycles, and Dad's thing was motorcycles when he had a day off. We'd go up through the mountains and he would carry me along and have me sit on the back for weight."

Doug's early exposure to stock cars helped him get into some of NASCAR's famed tracks when he was very young.

"I remember going to Darlington one year and it makes you really appreciate the motor homes," Doug says. "We would all sleep in vans and play out in the infield and hang out in station wagons and put the tailgate down and have cookouts and stuff. Those are some of the things I remember about growing up. He [Robert] would never let me go in the garage area, but Brad and Todd Parrott could go in the garage area with their dad, Buddy Parrott, who was a crew chief. . . . I do also remember getting in trouble for getting in the garage without a pass. I was probably 10 or 12 years old at the time."

Like his father, Doug has always enjoyed the mechanical things in life. Stock car racing has always fit the bill nicely. Doug Yates is the chief engine builder for Robert Yates Racing.

"I think it's partly because I went to school to get an engineering degree," Doug says. "I really thought I wanted to design cars . . . everybody has what they think is their ultimate dream. . . . The engine was interesting to me because I grew up around it, so it came somewhat easier than maybe other things to do with racing. It's been a neat challenge to take an engine shop and three or four guys, and with obviously a great teacher in my dad, and turn that into 60 guys. That's kinda of neat."

Along the way, there have been some hard times emotionally because racing is a job that requires its competitors to travel regularly. For a long time, Doug wasn't happy about that part of the business.

"(Stock car racing is) a great way to make a living and it's become more and more of a family sport, but when I was younger, Dad was gone all the time and I didn't really get to see him. The other dads were at ballgames and mine wasn't. It's probably not the best way to grow up. . . . I've been doing this full time for 10 years and if I wouldn't have done this, I don't really know what it would have been. If I hadn't done this for a living, I would have never been able to get to know my dad, who he is, or what he's about."

Working on race cars in the early 1970s wasn't as lucrative a job as it is today. There

Bobby Allison, the winner of 83 NASCAR Winston Cup races, enjoyed having Robert Yates build his engines while he raced with team owner Richard Howard and manager Junior Johnson in 1972. *Don Hunter photo*

were tough times amid the glamorous world of stock-car racing.

"My dad at that time was like any other mechanic or engine builder for a race team. He made a decent living, but it wasn't great." Doug says. "Everyone assumes we grew up with a lot of things, but we didn't. We shopped

Engines And Horsepower chapter two

Bobby Allison is at top speed at Daytona en route to winning the 1982 Daytona 500 with a Yates engine. *Don Hunter photo*

at Family Dollar and my mom worked at the A&P grocery store."

Robert worked with Johnson until October 1975. During Robert's time with Johnson, they enjoyed a lot of success with drivers Bobby Allison and Cale Yarborough. Allison won 10 races in 1972 and finished second in 12 more events. He collected nearly $275,000 in prize money, a highly impressive number in those days.

"Robert Yates is one of those really special people who developed a talent, who could get that extra little bit out of those engines," Allison says. "He's really been able to apply that to a lot of types of engines. He built engines for Junior when I drove for Junior back in 1972. That was the big-block engine and he did a really good job with them when others wouldn't touch them.

"I didn't always have the best engine every day, but I always had one of the greatest. Later on, he built the small-block Chevrolets, and once again, some days I had the best engine. Then he

40

Robert talks with Bobby Allison during the 1985 Winston Cup season. The two had enjoyed a championship together two years earlier. *Don Hunter photo*

[Robert] went over to Ford, and pretty soon his Ford engines were the best. He could always put that extra little touch to his work. He's a very likable person and someone who is very dedicated to the sport of NASCAR auto racing. He would always apply himself and was always successful."

Allison had also worked with Robert at Holman-Moody when he was driving for the Charlotte-based operation.

"Robert was one of the young guys back in the engine room and he worked on the engines, but back in those days Holman-Moody had different job descriptions and responsibilities. He wasn't yet to the front of the engine-building ranks. Robert was one of those guys who seemed to really pay attention to things and he got the opportunity to go with Junior before I did. He was there the first year Junior was with Chevrolet in 1971 and had a really good year with me in 1972. . . . He's a really good individual who has worked hard and has been very successful in life as well as Winston Cup racing."

Near the end of the 1975 season, Robert decided to join longtime engine builder Park Nall. But that all changed when Darrell Waltrip won a race for DiGard Racing on Oct. 12 of that

41

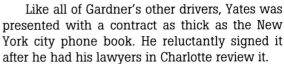

year in Richmond, Virginia. It was one of Robert's engines that propelled Waltrip to the win, and Digard wanted Robert to work for their team. Team owner Bill Gardner kept the pressure going, and Robert finally agreed to go to Daytona, where the team was based, to only help them get organized, and that was it. The outcome would be much different.

"Digard asked me to come down and stay two weeks," Robert says. "I told them [Digard] I was coming down to organize them. They had all kinds of people down there to build engines. That included Smokey Yunick [a winning team owner with his driver, the late Fireball Roberts], but I wasn't trying to straighten Smokey out. That was July 1976. I wasn't going to stay, but nine months later, I was still there living in a hotel."

Like all of Gardner's other drivers, Yates was presented with a contract as thick as the New York city phone book. He reluctantly signed it after he had his lawyers in Charlotte review it.

From 1976 to 1980, Yates built engines for Waltrip. In 1981, Ricky Rudd replaced Waltrip, and Bobby Allison took over at the start of the 1982 Winston Cup season. The engines that Yates built for Digard and drivers Waltrip, Rudd, and Allison amassed a total of 42 wins.

By the end of the 1985 season, Allison announced he was leaving to join Stavola Brothers Racing. Gardner had begun to experience financial problems, thus prompting Robert to look elsewhere for employment. Little did Robert know that his next venture would become his true racing home for many years to come.

In 1983 when he posed for this photo, Robert worked with NASCAR veteran Bobby Allison at Digard Racing. Thanks in part to Yates' engines, Allison won his lone career championship that season. *Don Hunter photo*

Far right
Bobby Allison enjoys showing off his championship trophy at the NASCAR Winston Cup awards banquet in 1983. *Griggs Publishing photo*

Yates stands in front of
Bobby Allison's wrecked
Buick during the 1984
Winston Cup season. Note
the young man with the jack
stand stepping over the jack
is Davey Allison. *Don
Hunter photo*

CHAPTER **THREE**

Joining Ranier Racing and Choosing Davey Allison

With Digard Racing in disarray after the departure of Bobby Allison at the end of the 1985 NASCAR Winston Cup season, the team's status as a championship contender was no longer mentioned as it had been in the past. Driver Greg Sacks had joined the team after he won the Firecracker 400 at Daytona in a Digard Chevrolet in the summer of 1985. Road racer Willy T. Ribbs was added to the fold, too, but success was never to come to him.

Robert left Digard to work with synthetic fuel research, but he wanted to be part of a championship-caliber team again, and when his phone rang with an offer to be engine builder and team manager for Rainier Racing, it was an offer he couldn't refuse.

Ranier had become a premier team with the likes of drivers Buddy Baker, Bobby Allison, Benny Parsons, and Cale Yarborough at the controls. Robert had worked with Cale Yarborough, the team's driver, when he was employed with Johnson. When Robert returned to Winston Cup racing, Yarborough was coming off the 1985 season in which he won races at Talladega and the fall event at Charlotte. Knowing the key players in the organization very well, Robert felt he was stepping into a good deal.

"After the Digard situation went away, I went off and looked at working with synthetic fuel, but I was still in engine work and did that

for three months. I realized I wasn't going to do everything I needed to do," Robert remembers. "I got back in the engine business doing engines for various teams. I was doing an engine a day and we were wide open.

"When Waddell Wilson left Harry Ranier's team, Harry called me and asked me to come to work for him. I told him I was just too busy to even talk about coming to work. The Ford guys had called, so both had got my attention, but I was still working night and day. They [Ranier] called again and asked if I would give them 10 minutes. So I finally agreed and we met at the airport. I ended up giving them two hours. They made me a deal that was not just lucrative, but it was also a chance to get away from working for so many different teams. It would also mean I could really work with a car. I could work with the 28 team and do all the engine work I wanted to do. I jumped into that deal and that's how we got together."

Yarborough ran 16 events in 1986 but could not secure any wins with Ranier's operation. By late summer, Yarborough met with Ranier and told him of his intentions to form his own Winston Cup team. Engine builder Waddell Wilson also left the team to take a similar position with Hendrick Motorsports owner Rick Hendrick. In essence, the team would have to be rebuilt from the ground up, which included constructing a

Davey discusses strategy with crew chief Larry McReynolds (left) and Robert in the garage area at Pocono in 1992. *Don Hunter photo*

A young Davey Allison talks with his father, Bobby Allison, and Robert Yates (far right) in 1982. *Don Hunter photo*

Davey is behind the wheel of one of his ARCA cars during the 1983 season. Ironically, his engines were provided by Robert Yates long before the two joined forces to tackle the Winston Cup circuit.

new Thunderbird body style that was introduced by Ford. Everything seemed in turmoil.

As team manager, Yates was asked to compile a list of possible replacement drivers, but another major problem developed. Yarborough was taking the Hardee's restaurant sponsorship with him to his No. 29 Oldsmobiles. Not only did Robert not have a top-name driver, but he also potentially had to go to the 1987 Daytona 500 and activities during Speedweeks with blank quarter panels. Rarely did such a scenario occur with a top-flight Winston Cup team.

Rusty Wallace's name continued to come up in conversation as a potential candidate to fill the driver void. Wallace, a St. Louis native, had joined the circuit in 1984 and won his first career Winston Cup event at Bristol International Raceway with team owner Raymond Beadle in April 1986. Wallace could bring enough talent and sponsorship to continue the team's reputation as the powerhouse organization it was known as in the past. Wallace was placed high on the list of candidates.

Another young driver being considered was Davey Allison, a standout driver who had won Automobile Racing Club of America (ARCA) events and entered a Winston Cup event for Junior Johnson in 1985 when he filled in for the injured Neil Bonnett (he finished seventh). He also entered a few races for Hoss Ellington, the team his uncle Donnie Allison had won races with, as well as the Chevrolets owned by Earl Sadler. Allison had been around the circuit all his life as the son of 1983 Winston Cup champion Bobby Allison. He had shown the Winston Cup fraternity that he had some natural talent to offer and that he could win with the right team.

"There wasn't enough money on the table, so we didn't hire Rusty for what he offered," Robert says. "To have Davey was a mixed emotion for Harry, myself, and everyone involved. When we finally said it was going to be Davey, we told him at Bristol in August 1986. He was the most excited kid I had ever seen. I knew we had our work cut out for us, and we did, but I knew we would be able to pull a couple of wins off every year.

"I had worked with Bobby Allison in 1972, and worked with him again in 1982, 1983, and 1984 when we won the 1983 championship with Digard Racing. I was around Davey all those years and he had won races with engines I had built for him in ARCA competition, so we already had this good relationship and I had been a friend of the Allisons since the early 1970s. It was just real natural because we knew each other well and had a lot of respect for each other. Davey had shown a lot of potential in 1982 in an ARCA car. To have him as my driver was the thing to do.

"When I went there to manage the Ranier team, I wasn't supposed to have to worry about sponsors. When Cale left and took the Hardees deal, we had the problem of no sponsor. To have Davey was a wonderful deal, but it didn't bring a sponsor. . . .

"The money that came with Rusty back then was something like $325,000, but Harry just blew that off and said we weren't going to do it.

Then it came back to Davey. He didn't bring any money, but he was definitely my first choice as far as being able to work with him. Rusty probably had more experience than Davey at that time in the Winston Cup. Knowing the guy personally, Davey was like my son. That struck enough votes with me to say go with Davey. . . . I don't ever remember having a bad time with Davey. We got along great. The fact that we were successful was probably as close as having my own

Davey Allison holds the winner's trophy after his victory in an ARCA event at Talladega Superspeedway in Talladega, Alabama. Allison's ride was powered with a Yates engine. *Elmer Kappel photo*

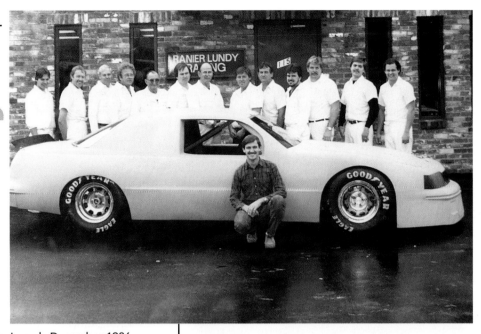

In early December 1986, rookie Davey Allison posed in front of a prototype 1987 Ford Thunderbird. Notice that the rear window is not yet cut out on the prime test body. Among the crew members standing behind, Richard Yates is positioned third from left, while Robert stands third from right in this Ranier-Lundy Racing photo taken before Robert bought the team. *David Chobat photo*

This public relations photo from 1987 shows Davey Allison's unmistakable grin after winning at Talladega that summer.

son do something. We weren't blood relatives, but I think we were as close as we could be."

Larry McReynolds, a longtime crew chief in the sport, remembers Davey from the days the two of them raced at Birmingham, Alabama.

"There was a point where I got to know Davey by watching him race at Birmingham, Alabama. You'd say to yourself, 'Man, how many times can this kid tear the guardrail down?'" McReynolds says. "He was the most determined individual, and I think one of the things that put the determination in him was Bobby Allison made him go back to Hueytown and put that race car back together himself. He didn't have 10 or 12 people working for him. . . . It was Davey who had to go back and put it all together, whether that was a front clip or whole body or whatever it was. Davey had to do it all himself with the help of maybe a few friends. . . .

"About the time I left Birmingham in the late 1970s you could start to see the true Allison coming out of him. He was a good race car driver who started showing patience and started winning some races. He knew he was going to be a force to reckon with."

In September 1986, Davey and his new crew chief, lifelong friend Joey Knuckles, came to Darlington to introduce themselves to the media in an impromptu gathering in the garage area. Dressed in a flannel shirt and jeans, Davey was smiling from ear to ear, and knew what an awesome and powerful team he had to work with. There was no doubt in his mind that he could win back the team's status as a winner.

"To be a part of Harry Ranier's team is a dream come true. Cale Yarborough has won races in this car, and I'm sure eventually we can do the same," Allison said to the small group. "Robert Yates is involved as team manager and engine builder, and having him as a part of the team says volumes. We don't have a sponsor as of yet but I'm sure we'll attract a lot of attention during the first part of the year—enough to get one. I wish we could start racing this weekend.

"Another big part of this plan is Joey Knuckles. I've known him since we were kids and I couldn't ask for a better crew chief. The team is starting over, but hopefully everything will come

together quickly. I'm real excited about joining this team."

After a long winter between seasons, Davey went to Daytona to start the 1987 season. Once he arrived in the garage area, he found his name on the roofline of a black, white, and gold Ford without a primary sponsor. The ever optimistic Allison knew it was just a matter of time before a sponsor would come. The best way to fill those blank spaces on the car was to have high-exposure success on the race track. Having the Daytona 500 as his stage was a perfect way to make all the pieces of the puzzle come together.

When it came time to run for the pole position, Davey turned in a speed that was just shy of Bill Elliott's pole speed of 210.364 miles per hour. He was only the second rookie driver in

NASCAR history to start on the front row in the Daytona 500. In 1976, rookie driver Terry Ryan started the 500 alongside pole position winner A. J. Foyt. In the Daytona 500 race that year, Davey lost a left rear tire just after making a pit stop and finished 27th. His performance was good enough to help land Texaco Havoline as the team's primary sponsor.

Three months after Daytona, Davey drove his Ranier-Lundy Ford to victory at Talladega Superspeedway after leading 101 laps (including the final 10 laps) of the 178-lap race. The race was shortened by 10 laps because the darkness did not allow enough time to complete the full 500-mile distance.

Davey's first Winston Cup win was just as sweet for him as it was for Robert, as Robert

Allison sits dressed in helmet and uniform ready for action in 1988.

Allison talks with Alan Kulwicki at Daytona in February of 1987. Davey was so new to the team, he didn't even have the proper uniform, but the hat proved he was with Ranier Racing. *Elmer Kappel photo*

had been right in choosing his young friend to handle the team's driving chores. Davey achieved a 21st place finish in his first year of Winston Cup racing.

"All in all, it was a great season for us," Davey said of the 1987 season. "We showed we could win some races and put Texaco Havoline up front. Being with this team is definitely a dream come true. I think the 1988 season will be even better. The more we race together, the better we become."

The win at Talladega may not have been taken as seriously as it should have been, as some may have suggested having run the final 10 laps would have crowned a different winner. A win at Dover Downs International Speedway in June 1987 helped make Davey a legitimate winning force in the sport. The icing on the cake was when Davey was crowned 1987 NASCAR Winston Cup Rookie of the Year.

The highlight of the 1988 season was when Davey drove his Ranier–Lundy Ford to a

Davey Allison

By the time this information card was published for the 1987 Havoline Racing press kit, Allison, a rookie in Winston Cup, had already accomplished quite a bit during his racing career. Statistics about Allison's Ford, the 1987 schedule, as well as information concerning the history of Texaco are also featured. The schedule begins on March 15 because Allison did not yet have Texaco as his sponsor for races at Daytona or Richmond that season.

HARRY RANIER
Car Owner

J.T. LUNDY
Car Owner

ROBERT YATES
Team Manager/ Engine Builder
Crew Chief

DAVEY ALLISON
Driver

A press photo sheet shows owners Harry Ranier and J. T. Lundy, with Robert Yates and Davey Allison in 1987.

second-place finish in the season-opening Daytona 500, a mere two car lengths behind his dad, Bobby Allison. It was the first time a father and son had finished a NASCAR race first and second since Lee and Richard Petty did at Heidelberg Speedway, near Pittsburgh, Pennsylvania, on July 10, 1960. Davey offered a few thoughts after joining his father in the press box for post-race interviews.

"I've got mixed emotions," Davey said after finishing second. "I had a lot of dreams when I was growing up, and one of them was to be battling my dad to the wire in a race. The only difference was I wanted to finish first.

"I knew my best bet was to help Dad get away far enough so I could protect second place and make a move if I could. I knew he had been watching how I passed everyone earlier. He knew my car was working really well on the outside, so there was no way he would give up the outside line. That's why he was up there between turns three and four. So I tried to fake that I was going high and get under him. I knew if I was successful, the only way I was going to win was by a few inches."

Bobby offered his version of the race to the press: "I think the reason I went up front as often as I could was my impression my car was the best one left. "Darrell [Waltrip] was strong, but I felt I was stronger. Then something happened to him and he faded. So my impression was to get the lead and not get hung up with someone in a fairly good car and get the sheet metal bent up. I saw the nose of Davey's car out of the corner of my eye, but thought I had enough suds to beat him."

To even have a shot at winning the 1988 500 was somewhat of a miracle. In the final practice session often called "Happy Hour," Davey scraped the wall and caused great damage to his Ranier-Lundy Ford.

"It was a mess," Davey says. "Among other things, it bent the snout, broke the steering box, and crunched the right-side sheet metal, but the crew is a great bunch of guys who worked late into the night to fix the car. It proves how tough they are, and I had complete confidence in the car. I think this proves this team is for real.

The Havoline crew is in action during a stop at Talladega during the 1987 Winston Cup season.

"Havoline Star" Pit Crew

Joey Knuckles — Crew Chief

Clint Ballard Tire Changer	Danny Ballard Pit Board	Stoney Ballard Radios, Tire Carrier	Devin Barbee Gas Catcher	Gary Beveridge Tire Prep.	Tom Ehret Gasman	Aaron Goforth Tire Prep.
Swede Hanson Gas Hauler	Larry Ifft Jackman	Hacksaw Knopf Gas Hauler	Tony Lambert Tire Changer	James Lewter Refreshment	Tony Price Chassis, Tires	Richard Yates Windshield

This public relations card from the 1987 press kit features the original team that Yates assembled when he hired Davey Allison.

Davey is all smiles from behind the wheel at Charlotte in May 1987. *Elmer Kappel photo*

Davey proudly sits in front of his new ride at the start of the 1987 Winston Cup season. He would prove he was up for the job by winning two races during his rookie season. *Elmer Kappel photo*

"We want to win the championship this year, and being second in points to my dad after the first race is a good way to start out. I just wonder what would have happened today if I hadn't wrecked the car."

Bobby grabbed the microphone from Davey and said, "Son, there are 29 more races this year to find out!"

Unfortunately, Davey's attention would turn to something much more important than the Winston Cup championship some four months later. On June 19, 1988, Bobby was involved in a near-fatal accident at Pocono International Raceway that eventually ended his driving career. As the

50-year-old former champion took the green flag, he noticed a left-rear tire was rapidly going down. After radioing to his crew that he was making an unscheduled pit stop after having to travel virtually the entire 2.5-mile distance on the track, he drove the bottom of the track at a rather fast clip.

As Bobby approached what is known as the tunnel turn of the three-turn triangular speedway, his car broke loose and hit the outside retaining wall. Seconds after he had come to a stop, the Chevrolet of Jocko Maggiacomo slammed hard into the driver's side of Bobby's Stavola Brothers Buick.

Bobby was first taken to the track's infield care center and then airlifted to Lehigh Valley Medical Center. Bobby's injuries included a severely fractured leg, fractured ribs, a fractured shoulder blade, and a cerebral concussion, which caused the most concern due to swelling of the brain.

Bobby's extensive recovery period took several months. Slowly, improvements came as he had to learn all the basic motor skills such as walking, talking, and eating. From a mental standpoint, years passed before he was able to function normally. Twelve years after the crash, Bobby still cannot remember winning the 1988 Daytona 500 over his son Davey or the near-fatal crash at Pocono in June of that year.

Different Times for Ranier and Yates

Behind the scenes at Ranier-Lundy Racing, the financial waters had become rather murky. Robert had been enjoying his role as team manager, but more and more the responsibilities were falling on Robert's shoulders. Cash flow coming into the team was decreasing, and payments to creditors were falling behind.

"I had sold my engine business [shared with Bill Gardner at Digard] and had taken the money and put it in the bank," Yates said in an interview with *NASCAR Winston Cup Illustrated*. "Ranier began to have severe money problems because of a divorce settlement and various problems.

"I had to pay tire bills, buy parts, and pay medical insurance [for the team] out of my

money. As it turned out, I was loaning money to Harry at a good interest rate. It was still Harry Ranier Racing, but I funded everything we needed to have. I loaned him a lot of money—$300,000 or $400,000."

Creditors kept the phone lines burning. Receptionists were quitting regularly, as they grew tired of being hassled for money. Carolyn Yates answered the phones and encouraged creditors

An artist's rendition of Allison and highlights of his No. 28 Ford filled the press kits early in his career.

Davey joins his father, Bobby Allison, in victory lane after finishing second to his mentor in the 1988 Daytona 500. It was only the second time in history a father and son finished first and second in a Winston Cup event. *Elmer Kappel photo*

to have patience. Ranier eventually came to Robert with bad news.

"He finally told me he couldn't make it and that he was going bankrupt," Robert says. "He split his partnership with Lundy. Then they were telling me I wasn't going to get my money back. That was very disturbing. I had already walked out on a deal that I had put 10 years into and lost $1 million and I didn't get bitter or upset. I just walked away from that. At this point, though, I was beginning to say, 'All this stuff is finally starting to get to me.'"

Yates had little recourse to recover his money. The majority of the shop's contents had been leveraged as collateral for outstanding loans. There was little that was listed on papers that hadn't already been held by banks around town. Yates' only hope was to find a buyer for the team. With that, at least he might receive a portion of what he had put into keeping Ranier's team afloat.

"Harry Ranier had been in the coal business and it just wasn't doing very well overall at that time in the late 1980s," Robert says today. "He

was trying to focus on that and he needed money. So I paid him out of the team and that's where we've been since then."

While conducting research to produce worth of actual assets of the team, Robert discovered that Ranier was asking $2.1 million for the race team. Lundy counteroffered at $1.7 million, but Ranier absolutely would not sell to his former partner. Yates, however, could offer the $1.7 million and the offer would be accepted, as long as Lundy wasn't part of the deal.

Early one morning in September 1988, Robert sat alone, his mind running as wide open as the engine dynomometers down the hallway. A good deal of his money was gone and was virtually un-recoverable. He found himself standing in a long line of people waiting to be paid. Davey came by the shop that morning to talk with the crew chief about some changes on the race car. As Davey rounded the corner, he found Robert sitting alone, and quiet with worry.

"Thinking about that team thing again, Robert?" asked the ever-positive Allison. "Look, you can do this! You don't need a partner. You've been in this a long time. You'll do all the right things. I'm planning to drive for you forever. Buy this race team. Like I've been telling you, you can do this! Don't think about it. Buy this race team."

Robert looked up and saw the confidence Davey portrayed through his encouragement. There was no doubt in Davey's mind what the next step should be. Slowly, Robert warmed to the idea and began the process for official transfer of ownership.

Ironically, Robert and Carolyn had made an offer on a house in Charlotte that was to be financed with a portion of the money Robert had made from selling the engine shop. With the money tied up in Ranier's operation, the offer was withdrawn. Had the offer been accepted and the money paid, Robert Yates Racing most likely would not have existed. The course of NASCAR Winston Cup history would have taken a much different turn. Davey Allison may have gone to drive for another race team, and Robert Yates would have possibly built engines as a hired employee and not a team owner.

Yates is looking up from his duties as engine builder in 1988. *Don Hunter photo*

Davey gets a beer bath from father Bobby Allison in victory lane at the conclusion of the 1988 Daytona 500. *Elmer Kappel photo*

On October 1, 1988, Robert closed the deal on the race team and became its sole owner. But to do so, the Yates had to sell virtually everything with the exception of the clothes on their backs. They were not only starting at ground zero on a professional level, but they were starting over on a personal level as well, much as they had done in the move from Charlotte to North Wilkesboro in the early 1970s.

Liz Allison, Davey's widow, still laughs about one particular gathering she and her late husband enjoyed during the Christmas holidays.

"I remember the Christmas party the year Robert and Carolyn bought the team," Liz said. "That was probably the loosest I had ever seen Robert. It was in their old house, the one they were moving out of. Things were boxed up everywhere and they were moving because they had sold the house to help raise the money to buy the race team. The big joke was, we have to sell the house to buy the race team, and Carolyn was saying to Davey, 'I can't shop anymore. . . . All the money has to go to the team. We can't do anything now because you talked Robert into buying this race team.' It was pretty funny. The talk was, 'Enjoy this party because there won't be any more parties for a while.'"

A New Beginning for Allison and Yates

Liz Allison wasn't completely accustomed to the life racing families have to endure. There were always scheduled appearances, autograph sessions, media commitments, and of course, a very hectic racing schedule. She soon realized how popular Davey was among his fans.

"I was so new to the whole deal [of stock car racing]," Liz says. "Tommy Allison (Davey's cousin and business manager) and his wife, Kelly, went with us. The excitement was just so unbelievable because Robert had finally bought the team. They were getting ready to go into a new season with Robert. I remember Davey was excited when we talked after the party. He was saying how joining Robert was the best thing that had ever happened to him on a business level. Davey was saying how he couldn't think of anybody in the world that he would rather work for than Robert Yates."

Upon the purchase of the race team from Ranier, Richard Yates joined Robert Yates Racing as its business manager after 23 years with Baker Equipment Engineering Company of Charlotte. With time, the financial troubles disappeared, past debts were erased from financial ledgers, and monthly bills were paid on time. Ricky Rudd remembers racing against Davey and Robert while with Hendrick Motorsports; he could see from across the garage area how tight finances were at times.

Davey Allison leads the field from the pole position at what was then called the Charlotte Motor Speedway during the Coca-Cola 600 on May 29, 1988. In the second row on the left is his father, Bobby Allison. That day, Davey finished 5th, while Bobby finished 17th after suffering a crash.
Elmer Kappel photo

Davey sits quietly behind the wheel of his Robert Yates Racing Ford in 1990.
Cindy Karam-Elliott photo

Allison makes a pit stop at Rockingham in October 1991. *Jim Fluharty photo*

Allison (center) confers with Raymond Fox III (left) and Larry McReynolds in the garage area.
Elmer Kappell photo

"At the time, he [Robert] was really sort of taking a chance with Davey Allison because Davey didn't really have a lot of heavy credentials behind him when Robert started that team," Rudd says. "Robert put the team together and Davey drove for him and it just worked. They didn't start with beaucoup money. I remember seeing some of their short track stuff and they would take the same car to Richmond [Virginia], Martinsville [Virginia], and North Wilkesboro [North Carolina], and there would still be a few scrapes and dents from the last time they raced it. They wouldn't even repaint the car. They would hammer the dents out and go on, but it always ran good."

During the 1989 and 1990 seasons, Davey was able to collect a total of three victories for the team, prompting the media to think of him as a strong threat to win the Winston Cup championship. Just prior to the Southern 500 at Darlington, South Carolina, in September 1991, Larry McReynolds replaced Jake Elder as the team's crew chief. McReynolds had been with the Kenny Bernstein operation with driver Brett Bodine and proved he could win races. In 1990, he helped Bodine win at North Wilkesboro, North Carolina, with a car that wasn't considered to be one that carried the highest sponsorship packages. There were four more top-fives and four top-tens; numbers good enough to get Davey's attention.

"Larry McReynolds came along in 1991 and we had it all clicking," Robert says. "We had a good car, good motor, and a good package. Everywhere we went, we had a shot at winning."

By the end of the 1991 season, Davey won at Charlotte in May (including a win in the Winston, a special nonpoints event); Sears Point in June (after being given the win when he spun after he and Rudd made contact in the last turn on the last lap); Michigan Speedway in August; Rockingham in October; and Phoenix the following week. There were also pole positions at Daytona, Richmond, and Darlington in McReynolds' first outing with Robert Yates Racing.

The Winston Cup championship was certainly on Robert's mind at each of the 29 races on the schedule that season. He knew his team wasn't completely ready to make a bid for it in its first few years of existence, but the potential was certainly there by the 1992 season.

"I've seen championships go away because a team tries too hard, doesn't try hard enough,

Davey Allison looks happy as the driver of Robert Yates' No. 28 Fords.
Jim Fluharty photo

Davey celebrates his Daytona 500 win in 1992. *Griggs Publishing Company photo*

"With Davey, we couldn't run good enough overall to even think about winning a championship when we first started. We would concentrate on the places we ran good and tried to pull off a few wins. Then, as we got things working for us in 1991—and Larry McReynolds certainly helped put things together in 1992—then we were running good enough to be in contention for the championship in 1992. In the last race of the season, it was all taken away from us."

The 1992 season began with Davey Allison and Robert Yates being touted as the team to beat before the season began. Those predictions weren't very far off. They opened the year with a huge win in the 1992 Daytona 500 over Morgan Shepherd in the Wood Brothers Ford.

"The Daytona 500 is a tough race to win," Robert says. "The way it happened was we won it with a back-up car. We wrecked the primary car and as it turned out, the back-up car was better than the primary car. We wrecked in practice on Wednesday afternoon, but we got the car going by race time. It was an awesome run. To win that race was great."

McReynolds stood in the pits hoping something wouldn't go wrong before Davey could take the checkered flag.

"I'll never forget those last 10 or 12 laps," McReynolds says. "I remember it was Morgan Shepherd in the Wood Brothers No. 21 car chasing us for the win. We didn't talk on the radio during that time at all, other than me radioing to Davey as to how many laps were left like, '10 to go, 5 to go, 1 to go.' Davey told his spotter to stay off the radio unless he absolutely needed to say something. He knew what he needed to do. I remember when he took that checkered flag—to know we won the Daytona 500 was something. Pretty much all the wins with Davey sounded like a kid at Christmas. He would be hollering over the radio about how we had won. At that point, you almost go into a state of shock.

"Davey was such a competitor, and I really thought he had a lot of years left. To win the Daytona 500 that year put us in an elite class. He never won a championship in any series. He had the chance to win the ARCA championship

or just isn't lucky when they need to be lucky," Robert says. "I would dream about winning the championship, but I didn't fixate on it. I tried not to allow myself to get up for it or talk too much about it.

early on but chose to skip the last race of the season to get married and lost that title. Just to have been able to work with him was very, very special and to see what kind of person he was is something I'll never forget."

What made the Allison-McReynolds relationship a magical one was that the two communicated so very well about issues concerning the race car, as well as topics outside the realm of motorsports. Davey and Liz were named godparents to Larry and Linda's children. The two were virtually inseparable and their respect for one another was quite evident.

"So many things happened in 1992, which was our first full season together" McReynolds says. "I joined Davey and Robert Yates the

fourth race of 1991 held at Darlington, South Carolina. We started the 1992 season by winning that Daytona 500, but there was a lot of irony to it. We tested quite a bit that winter. We didn't run very good during all the testing. The week before we were going to leave for Daytona for Speedweeks, Davey had to run the Copper Classic at Phoenix. We went to Talladega one more time and used up one more test. We were struggling with the car, and Robert was struggling with the motors. We just weren't hitting on what we needed to hit on. We had built a brand-new car for the 500 and used the car from the previous year as a backup car. Red Farmer did the test for us because, again, Davey was gone to Phoenix. Halfway

Allison's favorite position was out front, as he is here at Daytona in 1992. *Nigel Kinrade photo*

63

Joey Knuckles (left), the team's crew chief, walks down pit road with Yates at Daytona International Speedway. *Photo courtesy of Joey Knuckles*

through that test we started getting somewhere. We really had an awesome test with Red.

"We got to Daytona and really didn't set the woods on fire as far as qualifying. We had elected to run the same car throughout the entire Speedweek, which is unheard of today. That meant running what was then called the Busch Clash, the 125-mile qualifying races, and of course, the 500. We were really worried about running the Busch Clash with it because we were afraid we would tear it up. We came out of the Clash OK, but before the 125-mile races on Thursday, we got into a wreck and had to unload our back-up car. NASCAR was good enough to give us five more minutes of practice because it was that close. We just needed some time to check the car and run three or four laps

to make sure nothing leaked and everything was OK. We had a valve cover that was leaking terribly, so we were fortunate to have found that before race time.

"We got that car ready to run the 125s, and we worked late the night before and got in early the morning of those qualifying races. Because we used the back-up car we had to go to the rear of the field. We came back to finish third in our 125-mile race after starting dead last, so we felt pretty good about it. Had it been a longer race, I feel like we would have won the thing. We brought the car back in and tweaked on it Friday and Saturday.

"To me, the only bad part about winning the 500 really wasn't negative I guess. The four really good race cars to beat were Bill Elliott and Sterling Marlin of Junior Johnson's team, Ernie Irvan of the Morgan-McClure team, and Davey in our car. Right before the halfway mark, a big wreck occurred right in front of all four of them coming off turn two. Davey got through it and the three other guys didn't.

"On Monday after the 500, some of the media hurt my feelings a little bit because of headlines like, 'Allison's Biggest Competition Taken Out by Wreck.' We had already led a bunch of that race and it just kind of down-played winning the 500," said McReynolds.

Neither Davey nor Robert realized at the time of the win it was going to be a season of trials and triumphs. By winning races, Davey would lead the Winston Cup points battle, but when he wasn't challenging up front, Davey seemed to crash hard. His first injury came in the form of bruised ribs after a crash at Bristol on April 5. When he entered the event at North Wilkesboro on April 12, he was heavily taped and used an electric shock unit to curtail the pain. He led 88 of 400 laps and went on to win his second race of the season.

"All I was trying to do was start the race, run a few laps, and see how I felt," Davey said between smiles. "Well, once we got going, I forgot everything else except trying to get back to the front. Then all I could think about was trying to win the race. I'm sure I won't feel quite this good in the next couple of days. But

Allison's deep brown eyes usually told a story as he studied what mechanical changes the car needed in order for it to go faster.
Nigel Kinrade photo

right now, I'm standing here in a little bit of shock after this victory."

McReynolds saw a side of Davey that day that helped him gain a great deal of respect for his driver.

"That day was the day I really realized just what a special person Davey Allison was, especially with the fans," McReynolds says. "Here he had just won the race and gone through all the interviews in the press box. He's sitting there with cracked ribs and one of these electric shock units on to help stimulate the area and lessen the pain. He was hurt. You could see it on his face before he ever climbed into the race car. But after the race, after the inspection, and loading up the car and equipment, I looked out on pit road and there was Davey with probably 250 people around the bed of his pickup truck and he's signing autographs. That meant he was there until the very last person had

gotten one from him. The rest of these guys who were not hurt I guarantee were at home.

"Davey Allison, who was a lot like Bobby Allison, knew why we were there and why we do what we do. Without the fans coming to races to support the sport, we wouldn't be here doing this. He knew the true meaning of the importance of the race fan."

Having won the Daytona 500 earlier in the season, Davey was an early favorite to win the Winston Million if he could win two of the three coming events at Talladega on May 3, Charlotte on May 24, or Darlington on September 6.

Davey had many problems the following week at Martinsville, Virginia. He spun once in turn one and eventually finished 26th after an accident left him on the sidelines. It was a track that had also haunted Bobby Allison during his 25-year career in Winston Cup racing; it seemed to treat Davey just as poorly where luck was

65

Davey is all smiles as he prepares for the 400-mile event at Daytona in 1992. Earlier in the year, he was victorious in the Daytona 500. *Nigel Kinrade photo*

with the final two stops being for only fuel. The Goodyear tires shod on the spindles of Allison's Ford were wearing well and strong enough to hold up without changes the final third of the race. For Allison, it was a weekend where milestones were achieved. Davey's win made him the fourth driver to win the event three times, putting him in the record books with his father, Bobby, Buddy Baker, and David Pearson.

His victory in the International Race of Champions (IROC) made him the only driver to win in three divisions: NASCAR Winston Cup, IROC, and ARCA. The Winston Cup win Sunday brought forth an extra bonus of $100,000 from R. J. Reynolds Tobacco Company, in conjunction with the Winston Million. He was guaranteed the $100,000 because he had won the Daytona 500 in February and the Winston 500 at Talladega. To win at Charlotte at the end of May or at Darlington at the end of September would mean $1 million, the biggest payday for Yates Racing or Allison to date.

"I don't want to think too much about the Winston Million because I don't want it to take away from what we want—the NASCAR Winston Cup title," Allison said in postrace interviews. "That's the really big one. Sure, the Winston Million is a great prize to win, and to join Bill [Elliott] as the only winners of it in eight years would be a great accomplishment for the team and for the driver to look back at later, but our goal this year was to win the championship. That's the big apple at the end of the season. That's a million bucks, too, plus you have bragging rights over the rest of the guys for a year if you can win that one. If we were to win the Million, we'd be at on Tuesday morning to cash the check, but we really want the championship."

The next week in the Winston, a special nonpoints event at Charlotte Motor Speedway, Allison found himself missing from victory lane even though his black No. 28 sat there amid the hoopla. In a last-lap dash for the checkered flag with Kyle Petty, Allison hit the wall hard just after crossing the start-finish line amid a shower of sparks and heavy smoke. Allison suffered a bruised lung, concussion, and bruised knees. McReynolds remembers the evening well.

concerned. Only 16 points separated Davey from the rest of the field as they headed to Talladega Superspeedway, Davey's home track. It was time to get back on track after the humbling and expensive mishap at Martinsville that caused a 26th-place finish.

Davey was able to bounce back strong and put the Yates Racing Ford back into victory lane at Talladega, Alabama. He led the final 71 laps

Robert and Larry McReynolds are in discussion with Davey, who sits behind the wheel. *Nigel Kinrade photo*

The Robert Yates team studies Allison's moves on the track between pit stops during an event in 1992.
David Chobat photo

"We sprinted all the way down there and Davey was slumped over the steering wheel, and that scared me to death," McReynolds says. "He started coming to. I'm looking at Davey, trying to figure out what's going on with him. I'm also looking to see if they're going to put the No. 28 at the top of the scoreboard as the winner. Would it be 42 (Petty) or 28? At that point, 42 was up top because he had led the white flag lap.

"Finally, they get Davey out and I saw them flip the number. I said, 'Yessss!' . . . We had won

the race. We got that part done. They put him in the ambulance and he's halfway back now from being unconscious. Bobby Allison got in the ambulance with him, and I got in with him to go to the infield care center. At this point the phone in his head is ringing pretty loudly. Finally he said, 'What happened?' I said, 'You wrecked pretty big, but we still won the race.' Davey said, 'You're kidding me!' He asked me this four times about where the wreck happened. Each time, he would say, 'You're kidding me. You're kidding me.'"

Allison was carefully removed from the car and a precautionary neck brace was applied. Once he was on a back board, he lifted his right hand and offered a slight wave to the crowd. Unknown to them, much more had taken place during that uncertain time of trying to remove him from the car. Davey later told his wife, Liz, he thought he had a life-after-death experience during the crash in the Winston. He confided in her that for a few seconds he saw himself hovering over the grandstands and watched the rescue workers cut him out of the car. He later

came to and knew he was being attended to inside the badly damaged race car.

"We took him to the infield care center, and after all he had been through that year, that was just one more hard hit he had to endure," McReynolds says. "He basically killed that car. I went back to the garage area and there sat 007, all mangled and finished. It was our best car. Then it hit me that we were out of race cars. The car in the top of the truck had just been finished, and in fact, the guys in the shop didn't get it out there to us until Saturday morning, that morning

Davey (28) gets a bit close to Dale Earnhardt Sr. (3) at Charlotte in May 1992. *Elmer Kappel photo*

69

In a rare photo, Allison sports a beard at Atlanta in November 1992. *Elmer Kappel photo*

of the Winston. We didn't even have a back-up out there on Friday."

As a result of the crash, a rather strange but generous offer came McReynolds' way. "I was sitting there between our truck and the No. 11 truck, which was Junior Johnson's team that Bill Elliott drove for at the time. Tim Brewer, Elliott's crew chief, called me over," McReynolds says. "We sat there . . . just talking. We were battling Elliott week after week for the championship. He said, 'Man, you all did good tonight. I hate you tore that car up.' I said, 'Tim, we're in trouble. We don't even have a back-up car for next week.'

"He said, 'No problem, partner. I have a car at our shop that we haven't raced this year. Why don't you come and get it. You can paint it or you don't have to paint it. You just keep it as a spare. If you want to race it, race it. You just use it as long as you need to.'

"Now again, this was a team we were battling for the title. I talked with Robert and he said to do it. We got a car from them that next Monday, and we kept it in the top of our truck

Far left
A bandaged and bruised Davey Allison accepts the winner's trophy at North Wilkesboro in April 1992. *Nigel Kinrade photo*

71

Allison is all smiles after winning at Michigan in June 1992. Two months later, his younger brother, Clifford, would die after sustaining injuries in a crash at that race track. *Elmer Kappel photo*

the whole month of June 1992. We took it to Michigan, Pocono, and Sonoma, California. We didn't paint it. It stayed in the top of our truck with Budweiser and No. 11s on the sides. We had white decals made up after Robert got the blessing from Texaco that would have made the car a Havoline car with white 28s and white Havolines on a red body. The whole month of

June the top of our truck was a Budweiser car." The Yates team never had to use Elliott's spare car, and it was returned after the season.

Davey won at Michigan Speedway on June 21, and finished 10th at Daytona on July 4. At Pocono on July 19, Davey started from the pole position but was involved in a serious accident on lap 147 of the 200-lap event. While racing for position with Waltrip, the two cars made contact, which sent Allison into a series of barrel-rolls down the backstretch grass before coming to rest on his roof.

"We were both going for the same spot," Waltrip said in the postrace interviews. "Allison cut over and I slowed a bit. When he cut over again, which I couldn't conceive of him doing, I couldn't avoid hitting him. When I came around the next lap and saw what happened; it almost made me sick to my stomach."

For Robert and the team, there were several anxious moments because they didn't know if Davey was alive or dead.

"That was a real tough time," Robert remembers. "To start with, we had a car that could pretty much drive off from everybody. Darrell realized if he was going to get to us, he had to get to us early. He sort of went for him in turn one and missed him. What ticked me off was the fact it happened the way it happened.

"Again, I wasn't concerned about that part after I saw him roll and flip. I'm scanning all these other drivers and I'm hearing information from them and from NASCAR. It was bad. It was so knee-weakening; I don't know how I made it across the pit wall and started walking back to the garage. I went to where the ambulances come in. I'm still listening to drivers telling what they are seeing. That was tearing me up. The reports from those guys didn't look good. It's like seeing your worst fear unfold. You don't want anyone to get hurt, certainly not the driver of your own car.

"As the ambulance backed up to the care center, the driver gets out from behind the wheel and he says, 'He's going to be alright.' My mouth dropped because I wasn't sure if he would be alive. My knees got back under me and I started feeling better. His head was swollen pretty badly and his eyes were swollen shut and he had broken his arm. We immediately went into changing the cars around and tried to learn from our mistakes. I saw him in the infield and he really looked worse after they got him to the hospital away from the track. Knowing how many flips and rolls he took, he was really lucky."

McReynolds couldn't believe what he saw when Davey removed his sunglasses just after the accident occurred.

"He came to Talladega and got in the car when he wasn't supposed to. . . . I remember his eyes were really something. When he flipped his sunglasses up, his eyes had no whites. They were totally black. I've never seen anything like it in my whole life.

"The first thing he said was, 'I'm going to get that son of a bitch. I'm going to get him!,' talking about Waltrip. I said, 'Man, you ain't gettin' nobody right now.'"

Davey also endured two very personal losses in 1992. His grandfather, E. J. Allison, died of cancer on April 1. On August 13, his younger brother, Clifford, was killed in a single-car crash during a practice session at Michigan Speedway in preparation for a Busch Series event there.

"We were going to fly commercial to Michigan, so I left to get cleaned up so I could meet my flight," remembers McReynolds. "When I got home, Linda, my wife, told me I needed to call Libby Gant, the secretary at Robert Yates Racing. When I called her, she said, 'Larry, we're pretty sure that the report is true, but we think Clifford Allison has been killed at Michigan a few hours ago in a wreck in a Busch car.' Everybody was trying to find Davey to tell him. We finally had to get on the plane to go to Michigan. That night, we got to Ann Arbor where me and Robert were sharing a room together. We finally found Davey. He would usually stay with friends there and that's why we couldn't get in touch with him."

The pain Davey felt with the loss of his brother must have been tremendous, but his outward mannerisms proved to be the supporting foundation for grief others felt. His strength was incredible throughout such a horrible time.

"Davey was the one that got me and Robert back on track. Davey was tore up over the loss

Clifford Allison, the younger brother of Davey, prepares to take to the track during the 1992 NASCAR Busch Series season. Clifford Allison died in a single-car crash during a practice session at Michigan Speedway on August 12 of that year. *Tim Wilcox photo*

of Clifford, but he was determined to do what he needed to do. We offered to get him a relief to practice and qualify the car so he could be with family at such a terrible time. Davey quickly said, 'Let me tell you something. I'm up here to do a job and I'm going out there to win this race on Sunday. Then, we'll go home Monday and we'll bury my brother.' Not only did he have to live with that attitude, he also had to drive it through that very same corner lap after lap where his brother had been killed. He went out, still hurting from his own injuries a month before at Pocono, and qualified fourth and finished fifth. He drove his guts out that day and that's when it really hit him that the race was over and he had to go home and deal with Clifford's death."

On August 29 at Bristol, Tennessee, Davey crashed again and finished 30th in the 32-car field. At the Southern 500 in Darlington on September 6, the final of the four bonus races presented by R. J. Reynolds Tobacco Company was run. Davey had a solid chance to secure the $1 million bonus in the final race of the four-race contest. Several had tried, but only one driver, Bill Elliott, had been able to secure the bonus in 1985. As it turned out, heavy rain played a significant role in the outcome of the race.

Darrell Waltrip went on to win the Southern 500, the 84th and final victory of his career, and Davey finished fifth after only 298 laps could be completed due to bad weather conditions. Some miscommunications among Davey's crew

Allison is at top speed during a practice session at Bristol in 1990. He went on to record the win over Mark Martin in a photo finish. *Elmer Kappel photo*

Davey is on his way to winning the 1992 Winston special nonpoints event, as well as the $200,000 winner's share. *Elmer Kappel photo*

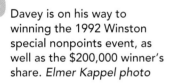

members seemed to help secure Waltrip's win. Robert recounts that piece of the team's history.

"We had an awesome race car, but it came down to a rain shower and how long that rain shower would last. Do we pit or not pit? Sure, it will dry up in a little while. So I say, 'Go look at the radar.' We sent a guy that had never flown on an airplane or never looked at one of the radar maps. . . . He came back and said, 'Everything is good, it's all green.' We rode this guy pretty hard about that for a lot of years. His interpretation that everything was going to be all right was that everything on the screen was green. We knew that meant rain was everywhere.

"We made a decision to pit and we didn't win the race. The rains came after just as Davey gave up the lead. We didn't spend the money we thought we were going to win, so it wasn't like we went home devastated.

"When we drove out of the race track, it was about as pretty of a day as you could imagine. There was still plenty of day light left. NASCAR said the jet dryer wouldn't start to dry the track, but we know it had Western Auto batteries in it, which was the sponsor of Darrell Waltrip, the guy who won the race. I've always said, 'Dadgum Western Auto batteries! We could have won the race.'"

Robert said his driver was ready for the rare challenge before him. He had proven he could win races and handle the pressure Winston Cup Racing offered.

"Davey was calm, probably more calm than I was," Robert says. "I just didn't want to mess up a good thing. I knew we had a good car. We put the number on backwards on the top of the car because Bill Elliott had won the Winston Million with the number done that way in 1985. Larry McReynolds wanted to do it. I told him I wasn't that superstitious, but I didn't want to be in the way of something like that."

With Davey's win at Phoenix, Arizona, on November 1, he was able to take the Winston Cup points lead. With 29 laps remaining, he passed Mark Martin for the win and held a 3.22-second lead at the finish. Allison held a 30-point lead over Alan Kulwicki going into the final event. Elliott, the third driver with a shot at the title, suffered engine problems all day and finished 31st.

At Atlanta, all Davey had to do was finish fifth or better and the championship was his, no matter what anyone else did. He was running fifth with 74 laps remaining when he was collected in a crash suffered by Ernie Irvan, in the Morgan-McClure Racing Chevrolet. Kulwicki won the title by only five points over Elliott by virtue of leading one lap more than Elliott. |Allison finished a distant third in the points race after being eliminated.

"Davey handled losing the championship that year with a lot more class than I had," says Liz Allison. "The year had been so up and down and emotional that when the wreck happened and took him out, I just went to pieces.

"I cried all the way to the infield care center as I walked along with Brian VanDerCook [then public relations representative for Texaco]. I was so disappointed for him [Davey] that I didn't want to face him. I thought to myself, 'God, he

Allison in his last year as a Winston Cup driver in 1993.
Elmer Kappell photo

has been through so much all year.' When I finally got back there to see him, he was so concerned about Ernie Irvan, to make sure he wasn't hurt. Here I had been angry, not at Ernie, but just the situation, and I thought Davey was going to be a hot head and fly off the cuff about everything, but he wasn't. He was so concerned about Ernie. He wouldn't even lie down on the stretcher back there for the doctors to check him out until he knew Ernie was OK.

"When we left there, he just gave me a hug and said, 'I'm sorry.' It was him consoling the team and everyone else instead of us lifting him up. He told me when we left that day that he didn't feel like it was Ernie's fault or anyone else's fault. He said to me, 'Liz, even if it was, there was nothing we can do about it. It's not going to change how hard this team worked this year. I've got many, many years to go for that championship and this was a lesson for me. It just wasn't part of God's plan this year.'

Allison is en route to a third-place finish in his final race at New Hampshire on July 11, 1993. *Jim Fluharty photo*

Robert Yates kneels down to the window opening of the No. 28 Ford to talk with Robby Gordon, the driver who took the wheel of the No. 28 Ford at Talladega the week after Allison died in a helicopter crash at the same track. *Nigel Kinrade photo*

"At the end of 1992, he was not the same man as he was at the beginning of the year. That whole year changed him completely. I think his relationship with Robert and the whole team was really strong. They had already become really close and they truly bonded with one another. This was a whole different level."

McReynolds summed up the year openly and honestly.

"We never even came close to getting on track after the Pocono deal," McReynolds says. "We didn't win another race. We were bobbling bad and so was Elliott, like neither one of us wanted the championship. Meanwhile, Alan Kulwicki was out top-fiving and top-tenning us each race. I think we had over 300 points behind us at one point, and when we got to Rockingham, he was right there. We took a new-style short track car to Phoenix and qualified OK. We weren't very good in practice, and with about five minutes to go in the final practice, we made a major change to the car. Davey said, 'That's what I've been hunting.' He backs that up with a win on Sunday.

"We actually lost the point lead going into Phoenix and took it back after Phoenix. We go to Atlanta with the points lead and mathematically, there were six drivers who could win that championship: Kyle Petty, Harry Gant, Mark Martin, Davey, Alan Kulwicki, and Bill Elliott all had a real shot at the title.

"We lost that championship because of inexperience on everybody's part. Robert had been with championship teams, chased championships, and won championships before, but Robert let us do our own thing. We carried the car we won with at Phoenix to Atlanta just because we won with it. It was the wrong car to take to Atlanta, Georgia. It was designed for Phoenix and Richmond . . . but it was wrong for Atlanta."

Davey's Final Season
In the first two events of the 1993 NASCAR Winston Cup season at Daytona and Rockingham, the No. 28 Ford seemed a bit off the mark. Neither race featured a top-five finish. The team did bounce back with a win at Richmond, Virginia, on March 7. Still, there was work to be

done if the team was going to get back to consistent winning form. Through the summer, this was an up and down season.

Davey scored four top-fives and six top-tens between the Atlanta race in March and Daytona on July 3. By the time the team reached the New Hampshire International Raceway on July 11, they hoped their luck would start to turn around.

"We had been struggling and hadn't been running good in a while," McReynolds says. "That day we figured out some things. I had changed some engine stuff from the first practice, and we changed some chassis stuff. Then we were in the hunt again. We led a lot of that race. We were so excited about running up front, Davey was actually counting the laps down on the radio. Somebody told us how many laps to go, but he corrected us.

"One of the caps off the hubs came off and they put the caution out after somebody hit it. The car wasn't as good on the restarts as it was on long runs and we got beat. We came out of there knowing we could win races. We were charged up and bubbly and talking and very happy because we thought we had turned our race team around."

Davey finished third and gave post-race interviews with a great deal of enthusiasm and confidence. He felt he and the team had found the missing ingredients that had eluded them during the majority of the season to that point. Late that afternoon, Davey asked Robert to join him in the helicopter back to Charlotte.

"He insisted I go with him in his particular helicopter [from the track at New Hampshire to the airport]," Robert says. "We got to his plane and I sat with Bobby Allison and we talked about a lot of old times. We were all in a really good mood. I remember Robbie, Davey's son, was helping him fly that night.

"I asked him [Davey] what he was going to do that week and he said he was going to fly his helicopter. He was an awesome pilot, from the time he was a lot younger. He bought this helicopter and I had already observed him flying a small helicopter, and it scared me. I'm not afraid of a lot of things, but it frightened me a little bit the way it maneuvered around our shop.

"I just said, 'Remember Davey, you've got plenty of money. Don't scrimp on that helicopter. You keep somebody flying with you until you get good at it. I've heard they're a little tougher to fly. Make sure you keep an instructor with you.'

"Davey said, 'Don't worry, Robert. I'll be fine.' We cared for each other. We didn't tell each other what to do because I wasn't his father. He respected me and if I had insisted on something, he probably would have respected what I had to say and done that. I wasn't a team owner who didn't let my driver drive other race cars. I didn't say much about stuff like that, but I did say this time I thought he should keep an instructor with him."

The next day, July 12, work around Robert Yates Racing was at a fast pace, as they were busy making last-minute preparations on the car they were taking to Talladega the following Thursday. During the three o'clock hour Eastern Time, an urgent phone call came into the switchboard in search of Robert.

"Robert, this is Bill France. Are you on top of the situation with your driver?"

For a second or two, Robert felt Davey may have said something in the newspapers that

Davey Allison (right) looks confused as longtime friend and crew chief Red Farmer asks him to explain the problems he's experiencing with his car. Farmer was with Allison when Davey lost his life in the helicopter crash of July 12, 1993. Farmer was seriously injured, but recovered. *Elmer Kappel photo*

Two weeks after his death, a sign posted by fans at Talladega Superspeedway praised Davey.
Nigel Kinrade photo

ONLY THE GOOD DIE YOUNG! THANKS FOR THE MEMORIES!

upset France. Robert was simply unaware of what France was referring to.

"On top of the situation with my driver?" Robert asked. "I'm not sure exactly what you mean."

"Davey has been in an accident with the helicopter at Talladega," France told him. "The situation doesn't look good."

Robert concluded the call with France and immediately walked out of his office. Many around him noticed the hurt and confused look on his face.

"When I got the call from Bill France, my knees just shattered," Robert says. "It was like taking everything you have and shattering it over your head. You have all these short-term and long-term plans running through your mind. Then, it's just a hard crash. It was as if everything I had was glass and it all broke. We were hoping and praying for Davey, but we knew it was serious."

Davey was taken to Caraway Methodist Medical Center in Birmingham. Over the next 16 hours, Davey's life hung in the balance. Medical procedures were performed to relieve pressure on his brain. Throughout the time he was in the hospital, he never regained consciousness. Davey's wife, Liz, was at his bedside, waiting for some sign that he knew she was there.

"I was standing at the foot of the bed holding his toes," Liz Allison explained in the July 1998 issue of *NASCAR Winston Cup Illustrated*. "I just started crying and said, 'I've got to know that you hear me. You've got to do something to let me know you hear me.' I was kind of getting to the point where, I loved him very much, but if it was time to let him go, then I would let him go. I stood there and rubbed his toes and said to him, 'Will you move your fingers? Can you move your hand?' His wedding-ring finger and pinkie finger moved. I then said, 'Can you move your toes?' He moved three of his toes. I said, 'Oh my God!'"

Liz ran from the room to find the doctors. She returned to the room and asked her husband to repeat the movements of his hand and foot, and he did. The doctor looked at her and said, "That's a blessing from God." At that point in time, Davey had no brain activity. At 7:00 A.M. on July 13, Davey died of severe head injuries as a result of the crash.

So many things were going through Robert's mind over the next few hours and days. It was as if everything were in slow motion.

"Me and Davey had done all this together," Robert says. "There were some good key people there, but your driver is a key part to that. At the time, we are thinking about next week or the next race. It just stopped when Davey died.

"I knew we couldn't race next week at Pocono. The next place was Davey's home. It took some encouragement and pushing from other people for me just to go race. The way it worked out, the people at Ford liked Robby Gordon and wanted him to do the deal. He turned out to be the perfect person. He certainly cared and all that. He helped us with our emotions because he wasn't close to Davey or the team. He didn't do everything right. That's how we got through that race."

Robert still thinks of his driver and friend often nearly a decade after his death. There are so many memories of the successes they shared together. This success was all because Robert took a chance on a young kid. What he found was a young diamond in the rough who was eager to make his name known in NASCAR Winston Cup racing.

"Like I've said so many times, Davey was like a son to me," Robert says. "He was a tremendous race car driver, but above that, he was my friend. Without him pushing me, I may not have ever become a team owner. He knew we could be successful and we were. We were able to win some big races together. Even though we never officially won a championship, there was no doubt we were a championship team. I still really miss him a lot and will never forget him."

Robert stands alongside one of his Ford in 1989 shortly after he purchased the team from Harry Ranier and J. T. Lundy. *Nigel Kinrade photo*

CHAPTER **FOUR**

Ernie Irvan

Upon the death of Davey Allison in July 1993, Robert Yates was faced with a tremendous dilemma in rebuilding the team. Having to find a replacement driver the caliber of Allison would be tough at midseason and there would be a backlash of negative comments directed toward Robert no matter which driver he placed in the car. Also, because it had been Davey's car, in the eyes of the fans, no one else would be acceptable. The fact that Robert had lost his close friend to a tragic helicopter crash had brought his world to a halt.

"I sat there thinking as I looked out the window, 'This is done. This is over with. This deal—no more.' Then I thought of my family I had to feed, and people who worked for us who needed a job. So I knew I should go on, but I thought I should try to retire this deal. I was mixed about what to do."

Unknown to the majority of the racing world, a plan was being conceived behind the scenes that would have rocked the sport at its foundation. Dale Earnhardt, one of NASCAR's greatest drivers, was set to take the controls of the Yates Ford, but would have to defect from General Motors, his sponsor with his present team.

"Not many people know this, but Dale Earnhardt came and talked to us about driving after Davey died," Robert said. "That would have put him back in a Ford instead of a Chevrolet, but we did talk about having him as our driver with Ford Quality Care as the sponsor. He [Dale] talked to me about the Quality Care deal before Dale Jarrett had it in 1996.

"Those talks were pretty serious. I think the number one was the number we had in mind. Richard Childress, Earnhardt's team owner, knew all about it. Before all of that could take place, Earnhardt and Childress renegotiated their contract and stayed together. For a time, though, I thought Earnhardt was going to be my driver."

With or without Earnhardt at the controls, Robert seriously considered changing every aspect of the race team. He didn't want it to be the same as it was when Davey drove the No. 28 car.

"I seriously started to change that 28 deal altogether. I even talked to Texaco about that pretty much in detail. I wasn't going to have a No. 28 Havoline car anymore. I had thought long and hard and decided that was it," Robert said.

Robert then began talking with various media members who had been covering the sport for many years. He needed advice as to what to do with his race team. Each time he sat and talked about the situation, he felt even more confusion, as there didn't seem to be an acceptable answer.

"Then, I talked with Bobby Allison (Davey's father) about it," Robert says. "He said, 'Absolutely not! Don't change that number or sponsor. You need to keep the 28 going. We want you to keep running the 28.' That's really all I needed to make up my mind as to what to do."

Robert decided to continue with the No. 28 Havoline Ford in the familiar black, yellow, and orange paint style that was adopted in 1991. The style of number did change, though. The round-style No. 28 was replaced with a squared and slanted No. 28. It was the same style Davey had used when he first joined the team in February 1987 until the 1991 paint scheme change.

Ernie Irvan has his helmet on and is ready for battle at Atlanta in 1994. *Nigel Kinrade photo*

A somber Robert Yates answers questions during a press conference at Darlington in 1993, the day he hired Ernie Irvan to be the permanent replacement for Allison. *Don Hunter photo*

Eventually, the decision about who would be the driver of the 28 car had to be made, and the choice was Ernie Irvan. But a huge problem threatened to road block the deal: An iron-clad contract had been signed with team owner Larry McClure that still carried several unfulfilled years on its pages. It looked as though all Irvan could do was stare at the No. 28 in the garage.

In the races between the July event at Talladega and the August event at Bristol, both Robbie Gordon and Lake Speed, as fill-in drivers, kept the wheels of the No. 28 turning. By the time the teams reached Darlington for the Southern 500 the first week of September, Irvan looked to have worked out the contract dispute with McClure and would be available to be contracted by Yates. "It was really tough leaving (McClure) because they basically had brought me from being an average Winston Cup driver to being a very competitive Winston Cup driver. We

had won our first race, and several races together," Irvan says

During the first practice session of the weekend held Friday morning, crew chief Larry McReynolds wasn't sure if he would have a driver. "I remember the car was sitting there in the garage area and it was getting later and later in the morning," remembers Larry McReynolds. "I honestly wasn't sure if we would have Ernie in the car.

"Then, just before the morning practice began, Larry McClure let him out of his contract. He did so in such a way as if to make Irvan sweat a bit before the release was granted. Once Irvan got his wish and ran to the No. 28 Ford as he zipped into Havoline colors, the smile on his face was as wide as the track surface he was about to circle.

"When he went out on the track for the first time and came back down pit road, he came to a

Ernie Irvan is all smiles as he
slides behind the controls of
the Robert Yates Racing
Ford at Martinsville, Virginia.
Nigel Kinrade photo

The only time Ernie Irvan took the No. 28 to victory lane at the Daytona International Speedway came in one of the Gatorade Twin 125-mile qualifying events of 1994. Irvan won the Daytona 500 in 1991 for team owner Larry McClure. *Nigel Kinrade photo*

Ernie Irvan makes a pit stop for a cut tire he suffered during the Brickyard 400 in 1994. *Nigel Kinrade photo*

stop and I knelt down to the driver's-side window as I did all the time with Davey," McReynolds says. "This time, when I got down to the window, I had the same feeling with Ernie that I did with Davey. I had a good feeling about where we were going with this. I knew Ernie was going to be able to get the car back up front and keep it there."

Irvan had completed plenty of Winston Cup laps to get to this point in his career. The Salinas, California, native had begun driving Chevrolets in select events for Marc Reno in 1987 with sponsorship from Dale Earnhardt Chevrolet, a car dealership in Newton, North Carolina. His first start came on September 13, 1987, at Richmond International Raceway.

Irvan then moved to the Chevrolets owned by D. K. Ulrich for 54 races and Junie Donlavey for three events before joining McClure late in the 1990 season in his 79th career start. He gave the Abingdon, Virginia–based team its first-ever win at Bristol in August of that year, and found victory lane again in the Daytona 500 in 1991. His career-best run at the NASCAR Winston Cup points championship was a fifth position that same year.

Robert Yates engages in an intense conversation with Ernie Irvan in the garage area at Atlanta. *Nigel Kinrade photo*

Irvan talks with Steve Hmeil during a break at Rockingham, North Carolina. Note the sign on the rear of the No. 28 Ford that sits right in front of them. *Nigel Kinrade photo*

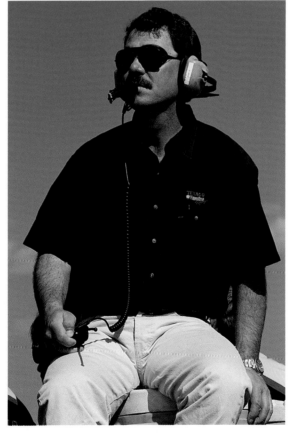

Ernie Irvan watches the action at Atlanta in March 1995 during his recovery period from his near-fatal accident at Michigan. *Nigel Kinrade photo*

While driving for McClure, Irvan found victory lane six more times. During his years there, he gained a reputation for being rough on the race track and unpredictable in close racing situations. In a class move, Irvan publicly apologized to his fellow drivers at the driver's meeting at Talladega in 1991 for driving rough in several races.

In his first outing in the Yates Ford at Darlington, Irvan came home in the fifth position. He was able to win twice in 1993. He had a strong run at Martinsville and simply blistered the field at Charlotte, where he led 328 of 334 laps.

The 1994 NASCAR Winston Cup season simply began under a dark emotional black cloud when longtime veteran Neil Bonnett was killed at Daytona International Speedway. Bonnett was practicing for the Daytona 500 when a single-car accident in turn four took his life. Two days later, Winston Cup rookie Rodney Orr was killed in a single-car accident during a practice session.

In the 1994 season, Irvan was jelling nicely with the Yates organization and placed himself in position to challenge for the Winston Cup championship, having won races at Richmond, Atlanta, and Sonoma. Going into the 21st event

McReynolds talks with Ernie Irvan (center) as Kenny Wallace listens to the conversation. *Nigel Kinrade photo*

Wallace studies a speed chart as crew chief Larry McReynolds (left) and crewman Raymond Fox look on. *Nigel Kinrade photo*

of the 31-event season at Michigan Speedway, Irvan trailed the leader, Dale Earnhardt, by 27 points. Before the weekend could be completed, however, everything at Yates Racing would change again by way of tragedy.

During the first practice session on Saturday, August 21, Irvan routinely strapped himself into the Havoline Ford and took to the track for a 10-lap run. He was running at 170 miles per hour when a right front tire was cut down by something believed to be on the track. Irvan locked his brakes and crashed hard into the first turn wall. Medical personnel were immediately on the scene and Irvan's injuries were life threatening. After several minutes, Irvan was extracted from his car after the roof of his Ford was removed.

"I was thinking, 'We can't be doing this all over again,'" McReynolds says. "'This just can't be happening.'"

(continued on page 92)

Ernie Irvan stands alongside the Robert Yates Ford just minutes before the start at North Wilkesboro in October 1995. It was his first Winston Cup start since his near-fatal accident at Michigan in August 1994. *Nigel Kinrade photo*

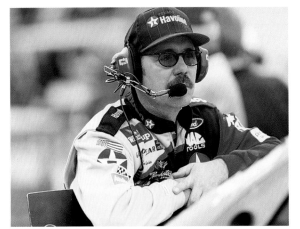

Kenny Wallace displays the Havoline colors of Robert Yates Racing as the interim driver while Ernie Irvan recovered from his injuries in 1994. *Nigel Kinrade photo*

While changes are being made to his car, Irvan grabs a team radio and listens to Dale Jarrett's crew at Martinsville, Virginia. *Nigel Kinrade photo*

Some days aren't as good as others. Here, the Robert Yates Racing team surveys the damage after Ernie Irvan's accident at Talladega in 1996.

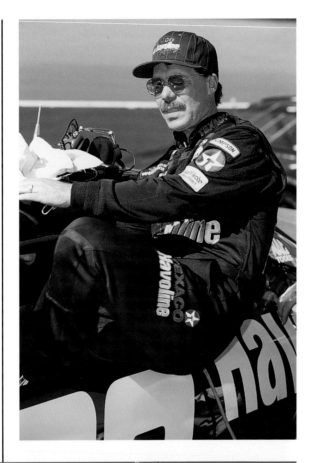

Ernie Irvan crawls behind the wheel of the Havoline Ford at Phoenix in late 1995. *Nigel Kinrade photo*

Ernie Irvan spends a few moments with crew chief Larry McReynolds in Atlanta in 1995. *Nigel Kinrade photo*

(continued from page 87)

"If you looked at the car at Michigan when Ernie wrecked, the car really didn't look that bad. The car Davey tore up in the Winston [in 1991] was torn up a whole lot worse. What really happened on that deal was this: Ernie had all of his belts on in the right place. The problem was he hit that wall with such force, [the car] just stopped. He stopped, but the parts inside his body didn't stop. The doctors will tell you a person's body just can't take that. That's why his lung collapsed and why he was injured so badly."

Yates elected to withdraw his team from the Michigan event, just as he did when Allison died prior to the events at Talladega in 1993. Irvan was hospitalized in an Ypsilanti, Michigan, hospital for many weeks after the crash. The initial diagnosis of Irvan's injuries gave him only a 10 percent chance of survival. Irvan survived, but his recovery would be a slow and painful process. His ability to regain normal functions such as walking and talking were very much in question.

Over the next 14 months, Irvan endured a slow and meticulous recovery. During that time, he watched Dale Jarrett wheel his ride to a victory at Pocono and log nine top-fives and 14 top-tens. Even though Irvan wasn't in a position to compete, it was good to see his ride continue to be successful. Few people gave Irvan much hope of ever returning to the controls of the Yates Ford.

"I had doubt," Irvan said of his chances of driving again in a May 1999 interview in *NASCAR Winston Cup Illustrated*. "The doctors kept telling me, 'Let's shoot for being able to drive your little girl to school. That'll be something that will be very rewarding to do.' I'm like, 'Wait a minute, now. I want to race again.' And they're saying, 'Let's just shoot for driving her to school.'

"Any time the doctors are telling you that, you have some doubt, but the human body is very much a miracle in its own. I know that I didn't do it alone. It was God being able to look after me and heal me up." Finally, on October 1,

1995, Irvan made a miraculous comeback at North Wilkesboro Speedway. He drove an identical red-and-black Havoline Ford that sported yellow No. 88s with Irvan's name once again stenciled on the roofline. Irvan finished in the sixth position after challenging friend and race winner Mark Martin in the Roush Racing Ford for the win throughout the 400-mile event. Jarrett, in the No. 28 Ford, finished seventh.

Irvan then entered the event at Phoenix, where he finished 40th in the 44-car field when his engine expired on lap 197 after he had led much of the 312-lap race. Irvan

Ernie Irvan battles Dale Earnhardt Sr. for the lead at Phoenix during the 1995 Winston Cup season. *Nigel Kinrade photo*

Ernie Irvan sported yellow No. 88s after he returned to the Robert Yates Racing Ford once his recovery period was complete. Here, he is shown at Atlanta in 1995. *Nigel Kinrade photo*

While in the garage area in Atlanta during 1995, Doug Yates (left), Robert Yates (center), and Ernie Irvan glance down at the engine in the No. 28 Ford. *Nigel Kinrade photo*

returned to the No. 28 Ford in 1996 when Jarret took the No. 88 and a new sponsor with Ford Quality Care. Irvan won two events that year at Loudon and Richmond to log career wins number 13 and 14.

The most well-known victory of Irvan's career came in June 1997 when he wheeled his Yates Ford to victory at Michigan Speedway, three years after the horrific crash that nearly took his life. With 24 laps remaining, Irvan pitted under green for two tires and fuel and only lost 9.2 seconds in the process. When all of the field had pitted, Irvan was in the lead by two seconds over Bill Elliott at the checkered flag.

"Being able to win here at Michigan, the last five laps my mind was going in all kinds of circles," Irvan said in the August 1997 issue of *NASCAR Winston Cup Illustrated*. "I kept going through turn two and kept thinking, 'Man, this is where the wreck happened.' Everything kept

Kim Irvan and daughter Jordan express well wishes to Ernie before the NASCAR Craftsman Truck Series event in 1995. *Nigel Kinrade photo*

going through my mind. It probably wasn't a good thing, because I was getting a little bit teary-eyed and it was making it hard to see. It's really hard to drive with tears in your eyes."

Even though the win at Michigan Speedway seemed to put winds back in the team's sails, there was still talk that Irvan and Yates would not be back together for the 1998 season. Yates confirmed that action near the end of the season and allowed Irvan to find another ride on the circuit. Irvan joined team owners Tom Beard, Nelson Bowers, and Reed Morton in 1998 and switched from Fords to Pontiacs. In his first year with the Mooresville, North Carolina, team he scored 11 top-tens and had 16 other events outside the top-ten with three races in the garage area before the race's end. Irvan was able to score three pole positions and more than $1,600,000 in season winnings.

Before the end of the season, Irvan suffered a severe crash at Talladega, which ultimately dictated his decision to retire from driving. Irvan made the announcement on September 3, 1999, at Darlington Raceway. A few days before Irvan's press conference, Robert received a phone call from his former driver, mostly just to talk to an old friend.

"He asked me if he could get back in the No. 28 ride, and I told him I just wasn't sure I could put that deal together," Yates says. "Then he asked me if I thought we could still win races together. I told him I was sure we could. He just wanted to make sure that was true in my mind and his mind that we still had what it takes to win. I told him I knew he still had it. I think he wanted to hear that before he finally made up his mind to retire from driving.

"We really had some great times together and some big wins. There was a time we could have won a championship. Then the accident happened at Michigan. I told him I thought it was important to be careful. I talked with him a couple of times by phone. He was searching for an answer as to what to do. He and I had a heart-to-heart talk. He finally said to me, 'I just want to hear you say you think I can get it done.' I agreed with him. He said, 'You know what, Robert? You and I can win races together.'

Ernie Irvan shares a moment with longtime friend Mark Martin at Talladega in 1995. *Nigel Kinrade photo*

Ernie Irvan stands alone atop the Robert Yates Racing transporter at Atlanta in 1995. *Nigel Kinrade photo*

95

Ernie Irvan looks toward the track during a weekend at Bristol, Tennessee, in 1996 as Dale Jarrett sits in the foreground. *Nigel Kinrade photo*

Announcer John Kernan has a word with Irvan before the start of the 1996 Daytona 500.

I agreed with him. I told him we could do that, but he didn't have that enthusiasm. He wanted to retire with him making the decision, knowing he could still come back and win. He believed that and I believe that.

"I didn't sugarcoat anything. I told him what was on my mind. What he was working on then was trying to make his decision, I think. Again, he has conquered everything, and in my mind, I could say he's the toughest that's ever been. I reserve the best for somebody else, but he's the toughest.

"He's got his health and had everything in place. He's financially set and I'm glad we all contributed. . . . In the long run, it's probably the best thing that ever happened to him, aside from all the people in Winston Cup racing who have helped give the opportunity to do what he wanted to do. He was a thrill to work with and quite a tough guy who loved racing."

Irvan's words were very sincere at the press conference as he addressed a packed room of media members and some of the competitors he raced for and against.

"I appreciate everybody coming out and this is really a special moment in my career. It is probably one that I felt I would never have to face," Irvan said. "I figure it is smart for me to retire. There is nothing that the doctors have actually told me. They just said that if I have another accident just like the one I just had, or had another one like in Michigan, it probably would be detrimental to me being able to live a wholesome life.

"I have two kids that are great and I have a wife, and they mean a lot to me. I have a great sponsor, M&M Mars, and all the people of this race team. They have really supported me and it is again something that brings tears to my eyes just knowing that I am never going to drive a Winston Cup car again. But I know it is something that I . . . cherish . . . what Winston Cup racing has been able to do to me and for my career, being able to be involved in it and with Winston, and what they have been able to do for the sport and NASCAR."

(continued on page 100)

To the amazement of both fans and race teams alike, Ernie Irvan was victorious in the 1996 Dura Lube 300 at New Hampshire and proved he could still win races. *Nigel Kinrade photo*

Ernie Irvan talks with crew chief Larry McReynolds (with back to camera) during a break at North Wilkesboro in 1996.

97

Ernie Irvan and the late Dale Earnhardt Sr. lead the field to start the 1996 500. *Nigel Kinrade photo*

Ernie Irvan leads the field at Sonoma, California, in June 1996. *Nigel Kinrade photo*

Larry McReynolds confers with Ernie Irvan at Martinsville, Virginia, in 1996. *Nigel Kinrade photo*

(continued from page 96)

Irvan took a moment to praise the track emergency staff of Michigan Speedway for saving his life during the minutes following his crash in 1994.

"Obviously, the race track [personnel] at Michigan [Speedway] saved my life. The facility they had and the people they had to help and how they were equipped with the doctors . . . really saved my life. Again, being able to win there, that was an awesome time for Robert Yates. Being able to win a Winston Cup race there and knowing I almost died at that race track. . . . They are the ones who helped me to have a future."

Media representatives asked Irvan who originated the idea to retire. Irvan quickly established it was his decision.

"It was soley between me and my family. No one really quizzed me about it," Irvan said. "Everybody who has ever watched me race knows I've

Ernie Irvan and Dale Jarrett take a few moments to discuss race strategy at the road course at Watkins Glen, New York, in 1997. *Nigel Kinrade photo*

given it 110 percent every day. Today, I don't want to retire, but it's the smart thing to do. It's the hardest thing I've ever had to do, but I don't know if I could survive another wreck like I had at Michigan. I appreciate everybody's support."

Irvan also thought back on his win at Michigan in 1997 as one of his crowning moments, proving to himself he could recover from the accident, return to racing, and win after suffering such a traumatic accident.

"To be able to come back and drive was a dream come true," Irvan said. "Winston Cup racing is something I love to do. My experience in Winston Cup racing has been very good. There's no doubt that I don't want to push the envelope. I proved them wrong when they weren't sure I could survive the first wreck, but how many times can I prove them wrong?

"The doctors told me there was no doubt the first time I came back was a full-fledged miracle. They kind of explained to me, how many miracles can you have? So that kind of woke me up. He just told me he wasn't sure if I could survive another wreck."

Irvan ended his statement by saying, "I've been able to win a few and lose a few. It's been a great career. I cherished the moments I had in Winston Cup racing."

Robert was grateful he was able to work with Ernie and proud of the strength and courage Irvan had shown through his time at Robert Yates Racing.

"Ernie was a real man. I will remember nothing but the good times. I remember him coming back and proving he could win races. The win at Michigan was the best win of my life. Having the burden of wondering if he could win after being hurt there was really great because he proved he could. He was hurt in our car, but like I said, seeing him win there at Michigan was the best win of my life."

During a quiet moment, Ernie Irvan sits inside his Ford and reflects on the day ahead. *Nigel Kinrade photo*

Ernie Irvan enjoys what he does best—putting his Ford out front at Daytona in 1996. *Nigel Kinrade photo*

CHAPTER FIVE
Kenny Irwin

With the departure of Ernie Irvan from Robert Yates Racing at the conclusion of the 1997 NASCAR Winston Cup season, Robert was faced with making another decision on a driver capable of returning the No. 28 back to victory lane. Day and night, Robert thought of the impending driver change, all the while knowing a wrong decision could cost him his longtime sponsor, Havoline motor oil, and ultimately, the team itself.

There were several capable drivers on his list who would bring a vast amount of talent with them. Among them was Wally Dallenbach Jr., a longtime Winston Cup veteran with former assignments with team owners Junie Donlavey, Jack Roush, Felix Sabates, and Rick Hendrick, to name a few. Dallenbach had made a name for himself on the SCCA Trans-Am circuit as that sanction's rookie of the year in 1984 and series champion the following year.

Also under consideration was Sterling Marlin, the son of former Winston Cup veteran Clifton "Coo Coo" Marlin. The Tennessee native had worked on his father's race cars as a crew member for many years and built his own driving career by winning the 1983 NASCAR Winston Cup rookie honors. He steadily progressed in machines owned by Hoss Ellington, Junior Johnson, Billy Hagan, Sabates, and Larry McClure. Sterling won back-to-back Daytona 500s in 1994 and 1995, as well as four other superspeedway events while he raced with McClure.

There was one other rising star who made his name known very quickly once he made it to the prestigious ranks of NASCAR. His name was Kenny Irwin Jr., an Indianapolis native who, like Jeff Gordon and Tony Stewart, grew up racing the fast open-wheel midgets and Sprint Cars around the Midwest.

Irwin's list of credentials was impressive. He was named the 1993 United States Auto Club (USAC) Sprint Car Series Rookie of the Year, the 1994 USAC Silver Crown Rookie of the Year, the 1996 USAC Midget Series champion, and 1997 NASCAR Craftsman Truck Series Rookie of the Year. The 27-year-old certainly knew the word *success,* and seemingly the last hurdle to jump would be entry into the NASCAR Winston Cup ranks. Irwin got that opportunity with team owner David Blair at Richmond on September 5, 1997. He rewarded Blair with a performance good enough to capture an outside front row start in his first-ever Winston Cup appearance, which resulted in a top-ten finish the following day. Three other outings for Blair produced two finishes well back into the field and one DNF (Did Not Finish).

The Havoline Ford had carried talented drivers throughout its existence. Davey Allison turned the wheels of the cars from the No. 28 stables as a rookie in 1987. After Allison, there were Irvan, Dale Jarrett when Irvan was injured, and now, possibly another rookie driver. Robert spent many hours deliberating over making the right decision. The driver who eventually would get the ride could possibly be locked into a long-term contract. That meant having someone who could get along with the crew and the crew chief without a hitch. Also, in order to keep every aspect of the arrangement excited, race wins had to come. Without them, the driver, pit crew, team owner, and sponsor would all have a very bad year. That was stress Robert simply didn't need. Finally, with some persuasion from Ford Motor Company, Irwin was given the nod to join the Yates operation as the team's driver of the No. 28 Ford.

Kenny Irwin talks with crew chief Doug Richert at Texas Motor Speedway during the 1999 Winston Cup season. The two enjoyed some impressive runs together. *Nigel Kinrade photo*

103

The late Kenny Irwin sits behind the wheel of the Robert Yates Racing Ford ready for the race to get underway. *Nigel Kinrade photo*

Kenny Irwin, who was considered a rising star in NASCAR, stands in the garage and sports the Texaco star on his uniform in this 1998 photo. The longtime sponsor has been with the team since 1987. *Nigel Kinrade photo*

There was a feeling of a new beginning with Irwin. Yates had taken a chance on Davey Allison when he was a rookie some 10 years earlier, so magic could strike twice. There were times during the 1998 and 1999 seasons when Irwin had good runs for Yates Racing. He scored three pole positions in those two seasons combined and won the 1998 Winston Cup rookie honors. He also recorded his best career finish, a third, in the 1999 Daytona 500. But in 67 events with Yates, there were only three top-fives and seven top-ten finishes. Also among those total starts for Yates, 43 fell into the finishing category of 11th through 40th position with 14 being listed as DNFs. In 1998, Irwin was 28th in the season-long Winston Cup points standings and improved that mark by nine positions to 19th in 1999.

From the beginning, something was missing. The much needed chemistry for a team to be successful in the ultra-competitive Winston Cup arena just wasn't there between the driver and crew. Personal styles simply didn't mesh, which caused discord and an overall lack of harmony. Because results on the race track did not live up to expectations, Yates and Irwin parted ways for the 2000 NASCAR Winston Cup season.

Looking back on the two seasons, Yates still respected Irwin for his talents. When Irwin left the Yates organization at the end of the 1999 season, he was offered a ride with the SABCO Racing operation owned by Felix Sabates. The change seemed to give Irwin confidence, a new start of his own, and another chance to prove himself.

In 17 starts going into the event at Loudon, New Hampshire, that was scheduled for July 9, Irwin was able to log one top-five and one top-ten with his best finish of the season coming with a fourth at Talladega on April 16.

When the transporters rolled through the gates of New Hampshire International Speedway on the morning of July 7, there was already some concern for safety. On May 12, NASCAR Busch Series competitor Adam Petty had been fatally injured in a single-car accident when his Chevrolet struck the third-turn wall at what was believed to be full speed. Speculation as to the cause of the crash spotlighted a stuck throttle,

Yates Racing drivers Kenny
Irwin and Dale Jarrett were
best friends when they were
on the same team during the
1998 and 1999 Winston Cup
seasons. *Nigel Kinrade photo*

Yates Racing crewman Jeff Clark, an engine specialist during Kenny Irwin's tenure with RYR, turns wrenches on the No. 28 Ford. He is presently with Dale Earnhardt, Inc. *Nigel Kinrade photo*

Kenny Irwin enjoys Dale Jarrett's company during a visit to Texas Motor Speedway in 1998. *Nigel Kinrade photo*

thus giving Petty no way to control his car in the few seconds remaining before the crash.

When Irwin arrived at the track, he visited and consulted with his crew and then talked with crew chief Tony Glover concerning the track and possible changes to the car. The mood among the driver and team was upbeat.

The lone Winston Cup practice session of the day began at approximately 11:15 A.M., as several cars left pit road. At 11:23 A.M., Irwin came off the second turn of the near-flat speedway and wheeled his car down the backstretch for the proper entrance into turn three. As he lifted his right foot off the throttle, the pedal remained flat on the floorboard, indicating the throttle had hung wide open. He locked his brakes, indicated by four dark rubber marks on the pavement, but no amount of brake is effective when a 750-horsepower engine is racing uncontrollably at full bore. In the short time span it took for Irwin to blink his eyes, his multicolored Chevrolet had made hard and vicious contact with the third-turn wall in nearly the same spot where Petty had lost his life.

The car's right side climbed the wall after impact and the motor continued to turn the rear wheels at full throttle. Finally, after riding the

Kenny Irwin makes a pit stop on the road course at Watkins Glen International in August of 1998. *Nigel Kinrade photo*

outside retaining wall deep into turn four with the driver's side scrubbing along the track surface, the car flipped over on its roof and came to a stop.

Rescue workers were immediately on the scene. Those in the garage area could do nothing but wait for word on their friend. From the impact Irwin had suffered, a dark and quiet feeling quickly overtook both fans and competitors alike in attendance at the speedway. The outcome didn't look too promising.

Once Irwin was removed from his car, he was taken to the track's infield care center. Many of the drivers went into the care center for word on Irwin's condition, but the stunned looks on the driver's faces told an all too familiar story. More than three hours after the crash, official word came from NASCAR that Irwin had

Crew member Raymond Fox III, the grandson of former team owner Ray Fox, takes a break with Kenny Irwin at Pocono. *Nigel Kinrade photo*

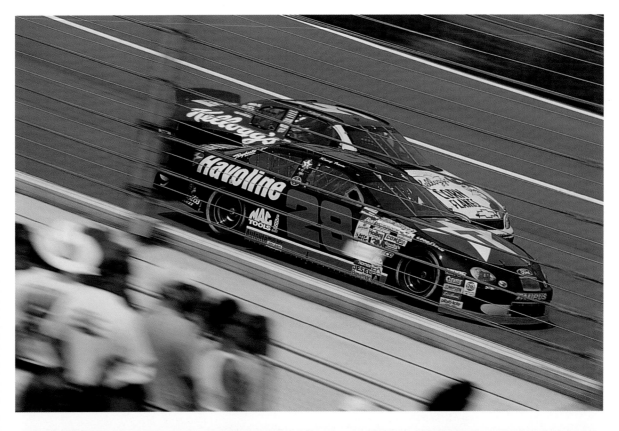

Kenny Irwin battles two-time Winston Cup champion Terry Labonte for track position at Fontana, California, in May 1999. *Nigel Kinrade photo*

Kenny Irwin became well recognized by fans as the driver of the Robert Yates Racing Ford during his three-year tenure. *Nigel Kinrade photo*

succumbed to injuries suffered in the crash. He had died instantly.

Possibly no one was more shaken by the news than Robert. There were times when Robert and Irwin had had personal difficulties, but Robert still had respect for Kenny as an individual.

When news came of Irwin's death, Robert removed his two-way radio headphones and found refuge in the team's lounge in the transporter. As he held his head in his hands, he tried to make sense of the tragedy. Moments after the crash, Robert said, "I wish that this didn't happen to our sport. I wish it didn't happen to Kenny. I wish it didn't happen for his family and his friends. I'm just sad. It's just a sad day."

Team SABCO also issued a statement and said, "Kenny was a great teammate and wonderful friend and we will miss him terribly." After the statement was released, the team withdrew the car from the event. They also covered the team's other car, driven by Sterling Marlin, and excused the crew so they could return to the hotel.

Crew chief Doug Richert (right) ponders the information Kenny Irwin has given him about the team's Ford. *Nigel Kinrade photo*

Kenny Irwin makes a pit stop at Pocono in June 1999. Pocono was the sight of some of the team's best runs. *Nigel Kinrade photo*

Kenny Irwin is preparing for the Winston Cup event at Bristol in August 1999. It's one of the toughest race tracks on the 36-race circuit. *Nigel Kinrade photo*

Kenny Irwin turns some laps at the North Carolina Speedway in February 1999. *Nigel Kinrade photo*

Irwin was a class individual. When reporters would ask him to comment on his years with Yates Racing, Irwin would smile and politely say, "I would rather not comment about the good things or the bad things. That was part of my racing past that I can use to be a better race driver in the future."

That Yates and Irwin never meshed as a successful team owner and driver continues to be one of Yates' biggest disappointments in his four decades of racing. He later reflected on Irwin as a race driver and as a person.

"I really wanted to keep a relationship with Kenny so I could brag on him one day that I helped him become a superstar," Robert said. "He showed a lot of talent. He had it. He just had to get the right equipment at the right time."

Some of Kenny Irwin's best races were at Richmond, Virginia, the site of his first Winston Cup start in 1996. *Nigel Kinrade photo*

CHAPTER SIX

Dale Jarrett *Joins* Robert Yates Racing

The moment Dale Jarrett drove his Joe Gibbs Racing Chevrolet under the checkered flag in the 1993 Daytona 500, he seemed to move from a competitor in NASCAR Winston Cup racing to a contender in a sport just ready to explode with popularity. The fact that he had beaten reigning champion Dale Earnhardt to take the win added further proof that he could come out on top against the very best.

Jarrett's long road to that jubilant celebration in victory lane began some two decades earlier on short tracks such as Hickory (North Carolina) Motor Speedway and Metrolina Speedway, located near Charlotte. Throughout his formative high school years, Jarrett was quite an athlete on the football field and basketball court. Aside from his stellar ability to swing a golf club, Jarrett's main topic of conversation was stock car racing.

In 1984, Jarrett got his chance to race in the Winston Cup in a Pontiac owned by Emanuel Zervakis for two events. Team owners Jimmy Means and Mike Curb called on his services for two more events before Eric Freedlander hired him for 24 events in 1987.

In 1988, Jarrett signed with team owner driver Cale Yarborough to share driving duties that year. To fill the void of not running the entire schedule with Yarborough, other entries came with Hoss Ellington for eight events, Ralph Ball for one, and Buddy Arrington for one. Yarborough, a three-time NASCAR Winston Cup champion in 1976, 1977, and 1978, was the only driver in the history of the sport to win three titles consecutively. After 83 wins and

more than 30 years of driving stock cars, Yarborough decided to leave the driving to the younger guys who had not had the misfortunes of the hard, grinding crashes that come with the territory. Yarborough retired at the end of the 1988 season and hired Jarrett as his full-time driver for 1989. That year, Jarrett finished 24th in the point standings after compiling only two top-fives and three top-tens. Sadly, his cars went to the garage area early on 11 occasions.

In 1990, Jarrett joined the famed Wood Brothers team from Stuart, Virginia, when their driver, Neil Bonnett, suffered severe injuries in a crash at Darlington in the spring of that year. The Wood Brothers had been a winning organization and a part of NASCAR since 1950, two years after the sanction was officially incorporated.

In 24 starts that year, Jarrett had only one top-five, six top-tens, eight events back in the finishing order, and nine events falling to DNFs (Did Not Finish).

In 1991, Jarrett enjoyed his first career victory at Michigan Speedway. Ironically, he battled with Davey Allison for the win that included the scraping of sheet metal before Jarrett was able to beat Davey by a mere bumper's width at the finish line. Even though Jarrett defeated Allison, it was a very well-received win among the sell-out crowd of 100,000.

In 1992, Jarrett signed on with team owner Joe Gibbs, a former NFL coach who had been victorious in three Super Bowl appearances with the Washington Redskins. Gibbs had tinkered with drag racing during his teenage years and

Dale Jarrett enjoys the spoils of victory after winning the Winston Cup event at Texas in April 2001. *Nigel Kinrade photo*

Dale Jarret stands alongside his Robert Yates Racing Ford prior to the 1995 Daytona 500. It was his first season as a driver for Yates. *Nigel Kinrade photo*

Dale Jarrett (right) shares a laugh with crew chief Larry McReynolds and a recuperating Ernie Irvan (center).

114

had followed the NASCAR circuit whenever he could find it on the radio stations or in newspapers. Gibbs wanted to do something other than football, and with his next love being stock car racing, it was a natural. Gibbs requested, and was granted, the number 18, because it was a number a football quarterback would use. His next step was to find his driver; Jarrett got the nod. In his inaugural season with Gibbs, Jarrett finished ninth in the season-long points race, and he enjoyed his highest finish at that time in the standings.

Jarrett went on to win the 1993 Daytona 500. It was only his second career victory, but to win the 500 places each of its winners in a very prestigious group. It was his only win that season, and the win surprised many of the media members who felt Jarrett and Gibbs might make a serious run at the championship. It would have to be a near-perfect season to offset the efforts of Dale Earnhardt, who managed to win his sixth

career Winston Cup championship. While driving for Gibbs in 1994, Jarrett and company once again failed to put together numbers impressive enough to win the Winston Cup championship.

Unknown to the large majority of the Winston Cup competitors, media, and fans, there were some huge movements being put into place that would change the entire complexion of the sport, and Jarrett would find himself at the center of those movements. Judging from the medical reports that were issued on a weekly basis, it had become obvious that Ernie Irvan would be facing a long, uncertain battle toward recovery. His was a day-to-day, step-by-step process with hopes of living a normal life. Driving a race car again wasn't even a consideration in the weeks following his crash at Michigan.

Dale Jarrett sits ready for the start of an event at Atlanta in 1995. *Nigel Kinrade photo*

During a rare break in the action, Dale Jarrett relaxes in the garage area at Talladega. *Nigel Kinrade photo*

Dale Jarrett Joins Robert Yates Racing

Dale Jarrett (88) and teammate Ernie Irvan (28) battle for position during a race in 1996. *Nigel Kinrade photo*

With Irvan unfortunately on the sidelines indefinitely, Robert needed a top-flight pilot with experience enough to put the No. 28 car into victory lane. Since the death of Davey Allison, the destiny of Robert Yates Racing seemed to lack stability where its drivers were concerned. Members of the race team were still recovering from the loss of Allison and Irvan's debilitating crash. Robert needed to deliver something positive to his team for the 1995 Winston Cup season. Once again, he had to start over with another driver behind the controls of the No. 28 Ford.

With the help of Ford Motor Company, the answer to Yates' painful dilemma was found in Jarrett. Through a mutual friend, Robert quietly acknowledged that he was interested in talking with Jarrett, and the two soon made contact by phone to set up a face-to-face meeting. When the two arrived at Darlington for the 1994 Southern 500 during the last week of August, they met briefly in the parking lot of the Raceway Grill Restaurant, located just outside the fourth turn (now the second turn) of the 1.366-mile speedway. It was a very simple conversation

116

Both Jarrett and Irvan paused to check out the lap times of a fellow competitor at Bristol in April 1996. *Nigel Kinrade photo*

DaleJarrettJoinsRobertYatesRacing

With Dale Jarrett's famed No. 88 in the foreground, the driver from Newton, North Carolina, reflects on his day ahead. *Nigel Kinrade photo*

that brought the powerhouse driver and team owner together.

"You want to do this?" Robert asked. "Yep," Jarrett responded. "Do you?" asked Jarrett. Robert responded, "Yep." They parted ways and the wheels of progress were quickly put into motion.

"The first time I talked with Robert about driving for him came by way of telephone conversation. Later, I guess you could say that was the face-to-face conversation we had with one another and talked about it and explored the possibility of what could happen," Jarrett remembers. "At that time, it was very premature because I wasn't looking to go anywhere, and he wasn't sure what his options were going to be. We did discuss it, and from there, things just kind of evolved."

Jarrett had always dreamed of having a race team built around him as the driver, in which he would be able to name certain personnel to have on his team.

"There were, I should say, certain scenarios that we talked about that interested me quite a bit. I realized going in that a year was probably what I was going to have there with Robert Yates. On the other hand, I felt like doing my own team was something that I wanted, and the proposal that was made to me was to help me with that in all aspects, so it was very intriguing to me."

Jarrett also knew there would be pressure in just having his name associated with the No. 28 Ford. It was a winning car and had been since Harry Ranier first hired Buddy Baker as its driver in 1979. Bobby Allison won with it in 1981, as did Cale Yarborough from 1983 through 1986. Then came Davey Allison in 1987, who amassed 19 wins of his own until his death in 1993. Irvan also took the car to victory lane in some high-profile superspeedway events. Jarrett knew he had to win in the car. If he didn't win, it could set his career in a

backward motion by giving him a reputation for not being able to produce when the win was on the line.

"There was a lot to live up to going to the No. 28 because of all Davey had accomplished in that car," Jarrett says. "I think other drivers have found that out since that time, and it's a difficult position to put yourself in. A lot of people might ask, why would you want to put yourself there? You just have to know Robert Yates and you have to know Carolyn Yates, and Doug Yates. If you don't know what a special family they are, then you might not totally understand why people are attracted to that operation.

"To get the call that Robert was interested in me was flattering. . . .It made me feel really good that someone of Robert's stature would consider me for his race car. It was also confusing to me because I found myself asking, 'Why am I getting this opportunity put in front of me? I'm happy where I am.' It gave me some confidence about myself.

"Even though at that point in time during the 1994 season we were struggling a little bit, I said, 'We must be doing something right to get Robert's attention here.' So it was exciting to think about the prospects, and when I told Kelley [Jarrett's wife] about it, we said, 'Boy, if that could just happen.'"

Jarrett makes his way by a slower car at Atlanta Motor Speedway in this 1996 photo. *Nigel Kinrade photo*

119

DaleJarrett Joins RobertYatesRacing

Jarrett proudly holds his trophy for winning the 1996 Brickyard 400 at Indianapolis Motor Speedway. *Nigel Kinrade photo*

Initially, the idea to join Robert Yates Racing seemed short lived. Jarrett had signed a long-term comittment to Gibbs just weeks before Yates presented his offer. It looked as though the contract would quickly stop the process.

"I realized right after being contacted that I had just signed an extension with Joe Gibbs, and all I can do is dream about this [to team up with Yates]," Jarrett says. "As we went on, we found out it was something that we could make happen. As they say, I guess the rest is history."

Jarrett was immediately criticized for leaving Gibbs' long-term arrangement to join a team as a fill-in driver until Irvan's possible return could be evaluated. In Jarrett's mind, there were reasons to look at joining Yates' operation.

"First of all, everybody doesn't understand everything involved," Jarrett says. "You don't know the inner workings of every race team and

Dale Jarrett is all smiles, with his wife, Kelley, by his side, as he holds his newly earned hardware high in the air. *Nigel Kinrade photo*

Two of Dale Jarrett's crew members push one of the engines to the garage stall for a change in the No. 88 Ford. *Nigel Kinrade*

The No. 88 team of Robert Yates Racing services Dale Jarrett's car during a pit stop in the 1996 Daytona 500. *Nigel Kinrade photo*

the dynamics that are going on inside and around [the team]. It's hard to look from the outside and understand all the reasoning as to why I would have a move like that."

Just after coming on board with Yates, Jarrett joined Robert and Ernie Irvan for a road course outing with some Ford executives. This helped seal a strong relationship between Jarrett and his team owner.

"This was January 1995, right before I started driving for him," Jarrett says. "I went down to Florida to a test track at Sebring. I was there to do some things that Ford was doing that wasn't with our race car. It was with some

test cars they had. We were just trying some new things. The track we used there was a road course.

"I drove some and Ernie drove some," Jarrett says. "Dan Rivard was in charge of Ford's racing arm at that time, and he was riding along with us. We had been keeping times. Well, Robert got behind the wheel and Dan was riding with him. I think Robert made it through the first two turns. There were trees in the middle and you just couldn't see turns three and four, but you could pick up watching the car as it came through turn five. So Robert goes barrelling through there and all you could see was a cloud

Dale Jarrett is well out in front of his teammate, Ernie Irvan, and the rest of the field at Talladega in 1996. *Nigel Kinrade photo*

The press is always asking questions, and Dale Jarrett is always willing to accommodate them. Here, he is in front of the microphones doing interviews at Rockingham, North Carolina. *Nigel Kinrade photo*

Dale Jarrett and crew chief Todd Parrott enjoy the moment after winning the prestigious Daytona 500 in 1996. It was Jarrett's second Daytona 500 victory. *Nigel Kinrade photo*

of dust. Robert had tried to go through there wide open and took a barrier as he went through. To see Dan come back in to the pits totally white in the face was something. Once we realized Robert wasn't going to hit that group of trees and had gotten back on course, it was just hilarious, but that's just Robert. He's so competitive. He was going to show me and Ernie how he was going to beat our times. He finally sat down in the back and said he would never do anything like that again."

Jarrett could only muster one victory at Pocono with Yates during the 1995 season. That fact only added more wood to the fires of the critics. Jarrett knew some time would have to pass before he and his team could gel as a unit. Quietly, he was helping his friend Irvan while setting a foundation for the future.

"Certainly, it looked as though we struggled through a lot of 1995, which was a very difficult year in a lot of ways," Jarrett says. "I kind of opened myself up for that speculation and second guessing.

"I had no regrets. Even if this thing had never evolved into the second team, I still had no regrets about coming to Robert Yates Racing. I learned a lot and I think I was better prepared as a racer and as a business person to go on from 1995 forward. As it turns out, things really worked out for me. There were too many things that were involved that people didn't know the whole story about. I knew I was opening myself up for criticism and speculation, which is natural. I was ready to deal with that.

"From the outside, you can say it's a well-funded organization," Jarrett says. "They have great engines and well-built cars. Aside from that, there's always that legacy of Davey Allison being there and what he did. You also have to look at how much he was loved. You're never going to get by that.

"I didn't go into that just as Ernie Irvan or Kenny Irwin or Ricky Rudd didn't go into that trying to be Davey. We all just went in there and tried to do our job. Again, to know Doug and Robert and Carolyn is to know a wonderful group of people who care very much for the people they work with."

In July of 1995, Jarrett finally scored that long overdue first win with Yates Racing at Pocono International Raceway. There were 9 top-fives and 14 top-tens that year, which translated into a 13th-place finish in the Winston Cup standings.

"It was a relief," Jarrett says. "To that point, everybody had won in Robert's cars. I didn't want to be that first one who didn't win in the 28 Ford. We had come close a couple of other times, but it was nice to get a win in that car and get that out of the way. I think that if it showed anything on everybody's part [it's] that when things weren't going as well as we had hoped . . . we all stuck together. Sure, we had our disagreements, but we worked through

Dale Jarrett takes a moment to sign a helmet for charity that was presented to him by a Sports Marketing Enterprises employee. *Nigel Kinrade photo*

Dale Jarrett hugs the outside
retaining wall to the delight
of the fans in attendance at
Darlington in 1996. *Nigel
Kinrade photo*

those. We were still working for a common goal and that was to get to victory lane and that was very gratifying that we could continue to work that hard with each other.

"By that time [the time of his win], it was a fact that Ernie [Irvan] was coming back. I was working on my own deal of forming the 88 team because that was the direction we were all going. To be able to work that hard and together, I think that said a lot for everybody involved."

Throughout the 1995 Winston Cup season, Irvan continued to recover slowly. He also continued to come to the race track, and acted as a consultant with the No. 28 team. It was rather awkward, as Irvan wanted desperately to return to his ride, but he was not physically and mentally ready to do so. Some people felt there was tension between Irvan and Jarrett, as the two had to adjust to such a tense day-to-day working relationship. Some felt Irvan was jealous of Jarrett's new role in Irvan's car. Jarrett looked at the scenario with a great deal of understanding.

"Ernie Irvan was in a tough position," Jarrett says. "He was there on the outside looking in

Ned Jarrett (left), a two-time NASCAR Winston Cup (then Grand National) champion, with his son Dale at Talladega in 1997. *Nigel Kinrade photo*

Dale Jarrett leads the field at Martinsville in April 1998. With many runs up front, there were signs that the team was moving closer to championship caliber. *Nigel Kinrade photo*

and that's always tough as an athlete. It's especially tough seeing someone in a position that you feel like you should be in. It's hard. It was rather difficult for him to sit and wait as long as he had to.

"A lot of things were said and made up about mine and Ernie's relationship that just were not true. We had a good relationship, as good as you could have with that situation. I think what it did was made us better friends and competitors as we got through that 1995 season. We became team members the next year, and

1996 and 1997 were two years I really enjoyed. Not because of the success we enjoyed, but because of Ernie, and being a friend of his and a teammate. I just enjoyed racing with him and learning from him."

During the winter months just prior to the 1996 NASCAR Winston Cup season, a brand-new race team under the Yates banner was being built from the ground up. Over a period of a few short months, a new fleet of Fords sat ready, painted in red, white, and blue. It was the moment when the plans Jarrett and Yates initially talked about

Crew chief Todd Parrott and Dale Jarrett share a laugh during a break at Dover, Delaware. The two have proven their close friendship can be quite effective at the race tracks. *Nigel Kinrade photo*

just over a year earlier finally came into fruition. As he toured the new 50,000-square-foot addition to the Charlotte-based facility, Jarrett realized he had the race team he had been promised when he took the role of relief driver for Irvan.

The final ingredient to the puzzle was the hiring of crew chief Todd Parrott; a longtime friend of Yates and Jarrett who had grown up in the sport just as Jarrett had. Parrott's father, Buddy Parrott, had joined the Winston Cup circuit in the late 1960s, and over a 30-year period worked with the 1970 Nord Krauskopf championship team with driver Bobby Isaac, as well as with Robert at Digard Racing with driver Darrell Waltrip. Parrott worked for Harry Ranier's team with driver Buddy Baker, and with Derrike Cope and team owner Bob Whitcomb to win the 1990 Daytona 500, and later with Penske Racing and driver Rusty Wallace.

Todd Parrott had been by his father's side during the years with team owner Roger Penske. There had been countless races where Parrott had worked on every aspect of a race car. All of that information was invaluable in his new role as Jarrett's crew chief.

"Me and Todd have a very special relationship as far as a driver and crew chief," Jarrett

Dale Jarrett dominated the 1998 Brickyard 400 until he found himself out of gas while in the lead. Members of both Yates Racing crews lend a hand. *Nigel Kinrade photo*

Dale Jarrett wheels his Quality Care Ford through the turns at the treacherous Darlington Raceway. *Nigel Kinrade photo*

Dale Jarrett Joins Robert Yates Racing

Dale Jarrett is all smiles in victory lane after he won at Talladega in 1998. The win gave Jarrett and Robert Yates a $1 million bonus to enjoy. *Nigel Kinrade photo*

Michigan Speedway was very nice to Dale Jarrett in June 1999. Here he is shown with Doug Yates (left), Robert, and Todd Parrott (far right). *Nigel Kinrade photo*

says. "One of the key points we covered when we started this team was we wanted to never get in a situation where we weren't having fun. No matter what was happening, good or bad, we wanted to make sure this was enjoyable to us."

Very little time passed before finding victory lane—they won the first event of the season, the 1996 Daytona 500. Finding success in their first outing as a team gave the critics little to talk about.

"I think our Daytona 500 win was looked at by a lot of people as a surprise, especially to win after coming out with a new race team that year with a rookie crew chief and all that, but I think that kind of solidified things," Jarrett said.

"I had won the Daytona 500 before in 1993 with Joe Gibbs, but I think that probably did give us a boost in the manner in which we did it. That probably did as much as anything to finally put Dale Jarrett on the map, but you have to look at the entire 1996 season. We won some big races that year. We challenged for the championship our first year together. I think that opened a lot of people's eyes."

Along with the Daytona 500 win in February came a win in the Brickyard 400 at Indianapolis Motor Speedway. Two more wins at Darlington and Pocono capped off a season with 17 top-fives, 21 top-tens, and a career-best third-place in the Winston Cup point standings. The success at the track was proof that the relationship between Jarrett and Todd Parrott packed some pretty impressive strength. Some members of the media had predicted in their first year that a championship would occur in just a matter of time.

In 1997, Jarrett exploded in the win column with 7 victories, 17 top-fives, and 20 top-tens. Once again, the numbers were good enough to name him a championship contender, but he fell one position short of the crown to Jeff Gordon.

In 1998, Jarrett won 3 events with 19 top-fives and 22 top-tens, and he also picked up a $1 million bonus from R. J. Reynolds Tobacco Company for his win at Talladega. In 1999, the magic that so many predicted finally came true. Jarrett and Parrott put together a season good enough to give Jarrett his first career Winston Cup championship, and first title for Robert Yates Racing. That year, there were four wins, including another victory in the Brickyard 400 at Indianapolis Motor Speedway. There were 24 top-fives, 29 top-tens, and he fell out of a race early only once.

Dale Jarrett is ready for action at Darlington in September 1999. It is one of the toughest tracks on the circuit. *Nigel Kinrade photo*

When all was said and done, it was Dale Jarrett who was crowned champion in 1999. Here he stands alongside the man who helped him get there, his crew chief, Todd Parrott. *Nigel Kinrade photo*

Dale Jarrett poses for photos in Times Square in New York City during his big weekend championship celebration. *Nigel Kinrade photo*

Far right top
At the NASCAR Winston Cup Awards banquet in 1999, the stage is filled with those behind the scenes who support the team so closely all season long. Joining Parrott is his wife, Debbie; Danielle Humphrey, Dale Jarrett's public relations representative at that time; Jarrett and his wife, Kelley; and Carolyn and Robert Yates. *Nigel Kinrade photo*

Far right bottom
The entire No. 88 team of Robert Yates Racing poses for a photo center stage at the NASCAR Winston Cup Awards banquet. *Nigel Kinrade photo*

After all of the hard work, the key members of Robert Yates Racing enjoy a special moment amid their championship trophy. They are, left to right: Todd Parrott, Dale Jarrett, Robert Yates, and Doug Yates. *Nigel Kinrade photo*

With his championship run, a personal milestone was established within the Jarrett family. In 1961 and 1965, Jarrett's father, Ned, had been crowned champion. The Jarretts were the first father-son combination to win championships since Lee and Richard Petty won championships in the late 1950s and early 1960s.

It was also something special that both Jarrett and Yates had won their first championship together. Their points lead was good enough to secure the title in the next-to-last race of the season held at Homestead, Florida.

"Obviously I was relieved that we didn't have to go to Atlanta and try to secure the

Dale Jarrett proudly stands alongside his favorite piece of hardware, the 1999 NASCAR Winston Cup championship trophy. *Nigel Kinrade photo*

1999
NASCAR WINSTON CUP CHAMPION
DALE JARRETT

DaleJarrettJoins**RobertYates**Racing

Dale Jarrett travels the backstretch at Darlington Raceway in March 2001 during the Transouth 400. *Nigel Kinrade photo*

The famed UPS Ford goes low in the first turn at Martinsville en route to winning the 2001 spring event at the 0.526-mile oval. *Nigel Kinrade photo*

championship there. We could just go to Atlanta and race. Back in 1992, Davey came very close to winning the title and got caught up in a wreck with Ernie Irvan when he [Irvan] was with Morgan-McClure.

"I think winning the championship at Homestead was a huge confidence builder for Todd [Parrott], Robert, and myself. I think the first thing that came to my mind more than anything else was the fact I was just really happy and excited for Robert and Carolyn Yates. That was the first thought—how happy I was for them.

"We had been close for a few years, but I felt like going into the 1999 season was the best prepared that we had ever been," Jarrett says. "When we started up in 1996, obviously we were starting something brand-new. In 1997, we were well prepared then and ran good from the start of the season. We lost the championship by 14 points or something like that that year. In 1998, we had to build a new car with

Jarrett's UPS Ford is quite familiar among Ford fans as well as the numerous fans of Robert Yates Racing across the country. *Nigel Kinrade photo*

the Taurus and got behind there. At the start of 1999, we knew what we had and we knew what we had to do. We got more prepared at the end of 1998 for 1999. I felt very good starting the season.

"Robert has always said he wanted our cars out front and let everyone else chase us. That's what you want to do. That's a tough position to put yourself in. You are looked at every week and everything you do is scrutinized. You have to be ready to perform week in and week out. It's a lot of pressure involved in that. It's something that has made me a better person and a better race driver and made me more appreciative of just what winning a championship is all about."

After 15 years of working hard to reach the pinnacle of his sport, it was an emotional day when he finally secured the crown.

"There were tears of joy," Jarrett says. "We were happy, and we had accomplished something that a lot of people don't get to experience. To think over the years of all the hard work and all the frustrations, and now to have a champi-

Zachary Jarrett joins his father in victory lane at Martinsville in April 2001. *Nigel Kinrade photo*

137

DaleJarrettJoins**RobertYatesRacing**

Right
Dale Jarrett (88) leads Kevin Lapage (4) at New Hampshire en route to another victory for No. 88. *Nigel Kinrade photo*

Below
Dale Jarrett shares center stage with a few friends after his win at New Hampshire in July 2001. From left to right are Whitney Yates (Doug's wife), Doug Yates, Jarrett, and Zachary Jarrett. *Nigel Kinrade photo*

Below right
Dale Jarrett shares a moment with his fans during a break in the action at Pocono in July 2001. *Nigel Kinrade photo*

Dale Jarrett is all smiles as he shares a laugh with crew chief Todd Parrott at Richmond in May 2001. *Nigel Kinrade photo*

Robert, along with crew chief Todd Parrott, joins Dale Jarrett in a victory celebration at Texas. *Nigel Kinrade photo*

onship trophy is really special. All of that [frustrations] seemed to come to an end with the Winston Cup championship in hand.

"Everybody works hard to try to elevate themselves as high as they can in their respective sport. We were able to do that. No matter what else happens or doesn't happen, we will always be Winston Cup champions. It's just a total feeling of accomplishment."

Jarrett often expresses his respect and admiration for Robert. There's no doubt the two will be together for quite some time, possibly even until Jarrett retires as a driver.

"It's unfortunate everybody doesn't get the opportunity to work with somebody like Robert," Jarrett says. "The things that make him the best owner [are that] he's a racer, he's a family man, he cares about his people. A lot of people don't get to see that. He wants to win more than anybody out here. He would only do it in a way where he doesn't have to

The Yates Racing No. 88 team springs into action at Pocono during a pit stop.
Nigel Kinrade photo

hurt people to get it. That's why people don't leave this organization. He is such a caring and wonderful person.

"You don't always see that side of him at the race track because what you see there is him being a competitor. He has a heart of gold and he's really good to all people he comes in con-tact with. He's a great friend and somebody I will always love and appreciate. That's for his talents but more for the type of person he is."

Jarrett has won the Daytona 500 twice and the Brickyard 400 twice. Add that to the 1999 NASCAR Winston Cup championship and one gets a feel for the success he has enjoyed.

Everyone is all smiles at the NASCAR Awards banquet in New York City in 1999. From left to right are Bill France, chairman of the board of NASCAR; his wife, Betty Jane France; Carolyn and Robert Yates; and Kelley and Dale Jarrett. *David Chobat photo*

"As I look back, I don't see anything that I would like to do over with this race team," Jarrett says. "I feel like we've all worked hard and worked in the same direction. Everything that we've done good and bad has been done for a reason. This is a dream team to me. We have the best engines and the best people working on them and the best crew members. This team is run by a racer. This isn't a side business for Robert Yates. This is his business and this is what he does for a living. He is one of the best leaders that I've ever been around. If someone asked me to come up with a better scenario for a driver, I couldn't. This is the best scenario."

Richard Yates (left) enjoys the Winston Cup championship celebration of 1999 with Dale Jarrett and Robert Yates at Homestead, Florida. *David Chobat photo*

CHAPTER SEVEN
Ricky Rudd

For the first five months of the 1999 NASCAR Winston Cup season, Ricky Rudd carried a huge burden on his shoulders. He needed an answer to what was the most important question of the season: Would his primary sponsor, Tide, come back to his team during the 2000 season. His crew was asking the question for the reason of job security, and Rudd himself needed an answer to determine the remainder of his career as a Winston Cup driver.

Finally, on June 30, Rudd came from his office, and in a quiet tone, comfirmed to his front office staff that the Procter and Gamble label would not be carried by his Fords after the 1999 season. It was a huge disappointment for the Chesapeake, Virginia, driver since he had been associated with them throughout his tenure at Hendrick Motorsports beginning in 1990.

It was no surprise that once the media learned that Rudd's team was searching for a primary sponsor, his name was automatically linked to Yates Racing as the pilot of the No. 28 with the certain, but unofficial, departure of Kenny Irwin.

Rudd was a high-profile, winning driver who had been victorious in some major events during his career, including the Brickyard 400 while driving his own Fords in 1997. Yates needed a veteran driver to put the No. 28 back into the win column. As one of the few winning drivers possibly available, Rudd seemed to be a logical choice.

Behind the scenes, Rudd worked diligently to find a new sponsor, and hoped to keep the doors of his Mooresville, North Carolina, shop open. Speculation among veteran members of the media, who had seen this type of development before, was that the two would join forces.

Rudd and Yates seemed like a perfect match in intensity and drive to win races. Because he helped make his own team successful, Rudd knew how to win under the toughest of circumstances. Privately within the organization, he was the leading candidate to replace Irwin.

Serious negotiations did not occur until after Irwin's release was announced in August. Ironically, the reports led Rudd and Yates to begin joking about his impending arrival. Rudd passed by the No. 28 garage space and threw up a hand. With the gesture, Doug Yates walked over with a request for his longtime friend to toss a joke his dad's way.

"We were at Indianapolis at the test session, and I was walking by their garage stall and started talking to one of their crew members that had gotten banged up at a go-cart race the night before," Rudd recalls. "Doug walked out there and said, 'You oughta say something to Robert about driving the car and make a joke with him.' So I walked by Robert and said, 'I'll be by there on Monday to get my seats fitted.' That's how it all got started."

Yates, however, didn't put the brief statements into any real serious context at first. The connection wasn't put together at that time.

"Ricky joked with me a little bit at Indianapolis and I didn't give it a second thought because I figured he's been successful doing his deal and it's not an option. So I didn't really go after it," Yates said.

With so much uncertainty revolving around his own race team, Rudd continued to pursue a new sponsor. There were people there who would lose jobs if a sponsor was not found. That was a point that was very unsettling to Rudd, as the members on his race team were obviously

Throughout a season of challenging for the NASCAR Winston Cup points championship in 2001, Ricky Rudd's smile never faded. *Nigel Kinrade photo*

In 1981, a young Ricky Rudd wears the Gatorade colors as the driver of the Digard Racing No. 88 entry, with Robert Yates as the engine builder. *Don Hunter photo*

his friends. To put them out on the street was something he wanted to avoid.

During an early-afternoon sports report on a Charlotte television station the day after Irwin's release was announced, an erroneous story had Rudd and Yates inking the deal. Rudd was home at the time of the broadcast and heard the report. It was that report that prompted him to begin seriously considering the Yates scenario. They had only joked at Indianapolis about joining forces, and neither had given the union any serious thought.

"It really didn't start until it was reported on the local news that it was a done deal," Rudd said. "We had not even talked. It was mentioned on the news and I got to thinking that it made a lot of sense.

"I was so focused on getting sponsorship that I was going to let that opportunity slip away. I

Ricky Rudd looks serious as he stands in the garage area at Rockingham in 1981. *Don Hunter photo*

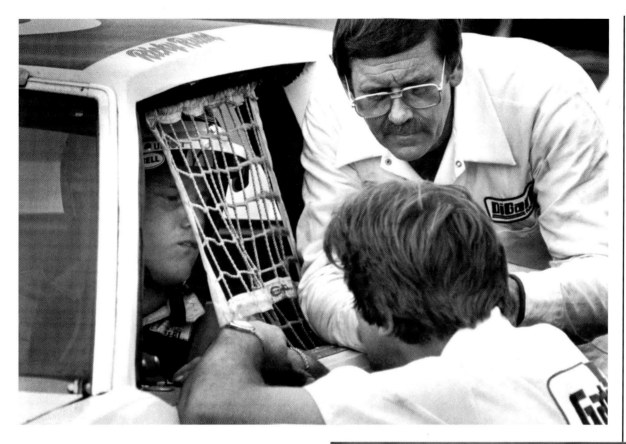

Ricky Rudd discusses the handling of his race car with Robert (at window) and longtime veteran crew chief Jake Elder (standing) at Daytona International Speedway in 1981. *Don Hunter photo*

Ricky Rudd finds himself among some of the best drivers in NASCAR in this 1981 photo. Ahead of him is the late Neil Bonnett (21), with the late Dale Earnhardt (2), David Pearson (16), and Richard Petty (43) trailing behind. *Don Hunter photo*

would not have recognized the opportunity, because I was 120 percent focused on finding sponsorship and didn't really think about the opportunity that was out there. That little media push is probably what helped make this happen."

As Rudd's hopes for a new sponsor began to dwindle toward the end of August, he finally called Yates and convinced him he was serious about driving his car.

"With the way sponsors were calling me and shopping, I figured he was not going to have a problem with sponsorship," Yates said. "He called me up and said, 'I don't care. This is what I want to do.' That's when I decided I want a guy who really believes in this deal. I don't want a guy calling up and saying, 'How much money can I make, what's our terms, how long can I drive for you,' and all that stuff. I want a guy who says we can work together and win races. He didn't care about how long we would race or how much money it was. He just wanted to

Yates leads the crew in extensive repair work as they check the damage to Ricky Rudd's Chevrolet after a crash at Rockingham. *Don Hunter photo*

Ricky Rudd is all business dressed in the orange and white team colors of his own racing operation before joining Yates in 2000. *Jim Fluharty photo*

drive the car. I put him on the list when he said, 'I can win races in that car.' He knows how to win, and he knows how to win at every single race track. That's hard to come by these days, and we're happy to have that."

Rudd continued to talk with potential sponsors, but the bottom-line number simply didn't meet those needed to win races. He had already been searching for a win all season to keep his streak of one win per season since 1983 alive. For the first time in 18 years, it looked as though it would come to an end at 20 total career victories.

Being a driver-owner, all of the problems rested on Rudd's shoulders. The level of competition has often kept the driver so busy keeping the team operating successfully that the performances on the track seem to suffer.

The part of the Yates deal that appealed the most to Rudd was that if he got the No. 28 ride, the No. 88 Yates team was most likely to win the 1999 championship. The more he thought of the

Ricky Rudd puts the Texaco Star through its paces at Martinsville en route to a second-place finish behind teammate Dale Jarrett. *Nigel Kinrade photo*

Ricky Rudd starts from the pole position at Darlington Raceway, where he eventually finished eighth. *Nigel Kinrade photo*

pros and cons of joining Yates, the longer the "pros" side of the yellow legal pad became.

"By just sitting back one day and mentally taking myself out of the ownership role and evaluating it as an outsider, I said, 'What would be the smart thing for me to do?'" Rudd says. "I started looking at it like, 'What do I really want to accomplish?' Right now, I really want to win races. I want to win championships. Can I do it with my own team? Well, maybe eventually. We've won some races, but a championship is two or three years down the road, maybe, if I get the right people. The 28 team is ready now. All the tools are in place. They've got everything it takes."

On the "cons" side of the sheet, Rudd had been down the road of a multicar operation when he drove for Rick Hendrick from 1990 through 1993. At that time in NASCAR Winston Cup history, the cycle of having more than one team did not always function successfully. Rudd desperately wanted a championship to his credit, and having the No. 28 under him would

The Yates racing crew springs into action during a pit stop at Talladega in April 2001. *Nigel Kinrade photo*

Ricky Rudd is all smiles at Pocono in June 2001. He went on to record the first win since 1997 for the No. 28 team that weekend. *Nigel Kinrade photo*

most certainly be his best chance. Yates and the No. 28 Ford might be the only combination to make the scenario work.

"That [was] one of the big motivations for taking the 28 ride," Rudd says. "I'll be honest with you, if the 28 team wasn't here . . . the reason, way back, when I was with Hendrick's in the early 1990s, the multicar team concept wasn't really working and going like I'm sure even Rick Hendrick would have anticipated it should go, and even like I didn't want it to go. It wasn't going very well. In fact, it took Ray Evernham to step in and get that operation pulled together. So, at that time, multicar ownership wasn't really the way to go.

"Teams like Robert's were not available. You had Davey that was gonna be there for a lifetime; so basically, I made a commitment I wanted to build a championship team. If I couldn't drive for one, then I'd go build one, so for six years I've been trying to build one and haven't done it yet. Now the 28 ride opens up. Had that 28 ride not opened up, I probably would have rode the sponsorship thing farther, and if nothing would have come about, I would have sat out a year until hopefully something came up that you could win the championship with. Like I say, this is a rare opportunity to have this open up for a driver."

Rudd had been very close to winning the Winston Cup championship in 1991 with Hendrick, but fell short to Dale Earnhardt. It was his last real shot at winning the title until he saw his name etched on the roofline of the red-and-black Yates Ford.

"I'm mentally seasoned for what it takes to hopefully try to win a championship," Rudd says. "In 1991 I came close and I finished second. . . . In 1994 I started my own team, and not to beat up on what we've done, we've accomplished a lot, but you can't start up a team and expect to challenge for a championship in year one, two, or three. So I've kind of been building and rebuilding.

"Every time we get good people, people would tend to hire them away. Then you're starting to build people again. We never had the financial backing it took to keep the thing solid and uniform. We were doing it on half the money that these other people have been doing it on."

Ricky Rudd enjoys the victory lane celebration with Robert (in black shirt) and crew chief Michael McSwaim (left). *Nigel Kinrade photo*

Ricky Rudd is on his way to win at Pocono. *Nigel Kinrade photo*

The Havoline crew performs lightning-fast pit stops at Pocono, which help to ensure Ricky Rudd's victory. *Nigel Kinrade photo*

RickyRudd chapter seven

Ricky Rudd leads Jeff Burton (99) and Joe Nemechek (33) at Martinsville in April 2001.
Nigel Kinrade photo

When one looks at Rudd's mission statement concerning his current three-year committment with Yates, the message conveyed is very easy to follow.

"I'm not looking for an easy road [and] I'm not looking for somewhere to go ride around and finish laps," Rudd says. "I'm looking for somebody that wants to put the same time and dedication into it that I am as a driver from the team side. . . . Who are the real racers left in this sport? You've got Childress and Robert, but you've got a small handful of guys that are really racers running these teams, so I'm not looking for an easy road. It's gonna be tough. I'm sure I'm gonna get my butt chewed out on many a day, but I want that. I want someone to say, 'Hey, you're not getting the job done. You need to go out there and push the button harder or you're not driving hard enough.' I'm ready for that."

Ricky Rudd brings the Yates Racing No. 28 down pit road at Sears Point in June 2001. *Nigel Kinrade photo*

Crew members of Digard Racing send Ricky Rudd back into action at Dover after a pit stop. *Don Hunter photo*

Epilogue

At the start of the 2001 NASCAR Winston Cup season, Dale Jarrett's No. 88 Fords began carrying the UPS brown-white-and-yellow paint scheme. The past red, white, and blue of Ford Quality Care that Jarrett had carried since 1996 were revamped to red, black, and white, and given to the famed Wood Brothers team of Stuart, Virginia, with the word *Motorcraft* emblazoned on the rear quarter panels and hood.

Jarrett, the defending Winston Cup champion in 2000, logged two victories coming into the season-opening Daytona 500 at the event at Rockingham, North Carolina, in October. Throughout the season, Jarrett was able to log 3 second-place finishes, 1 third, 5 fourths, and 4 fifths, with a total of 24 top-ten finishes overall. Jarrett posted a fourth-place finish in the season-long Winston Cup points race.

Doug Yates (left) joins Dale Jarrett and Carolyn and Robert Yates around the 1999 NASCAR Winston Cup championship trophy. *David Chobat photo*

Robert shares a laugh with wife Carolyn at one of the Winston Cup tracks on the circuit. *David Chobat photo*

Doug Yates stands alongside one of the many engines that have powered Yates Racing drivers to success. *Courtesy of Robert Yates Racing*

Doug Yates takes a glance at the leader board during an event at Lowe's Motor Speedway. *Courtesy of Robert Yates Racing*

Ricky Rudd began his second year with Yates Racing in 2001 and still carried the familar red-yellow-and-black Ford Tauruses. Rudd was unable to finish victory lane in 2000 but came very close to a win at Phoenix before he was involved in a multicar crash not of his making. Rudd logged one second-place finish at Michigan in August, was third five times, fourth three times, and fifth three times. Rudd also scored 19 top-tens and finished fifth in the season-long Winston Cup points race.

Robert and Doug Yates continue to provide engines for other Winston Cup race teams. Robert Yates Racing is still looked upon as a prosperous, championship organization with both teams being considered strong threats to win each week in the 38-race Winston Cup schedule. Without the contributions of so many, Robert Yates Racing simply could not have managed to become the powerhouse racing entity that it is.

Index

1071 World 000, 35
Allison, Bobby, 30, 34, 39–43, 45, 46, 56, 58
Allison, Clifford, 72
Allison, Davey, 43, 46–48, 52, 53, 56,   58
Allison, Donnie, 47
Allison, Liz, 58, 69, 75, 78
Allison, Tommy, 58
Allman, Bill, 33
Allman, Bud, 33
Altanta Motor Speedway, 119
Asheville-Weaverville Speedway, 23
Automobile Racing Club of America (ARCA), 47
Baker, Buck, 17
Baker, Buddy, 17, 21, 45
Ball, Ralph, 113
Beard, Tom, 95
Blair, David, 103
Bonnett, Neil, 47, 86, 113, 145
Bowers, Nelson, 95
Brady, Martha Yates, 13
Brewer, Tim, 71
Brickyard 400, 84, 120, 131, 133, 140
Bristol International Raceway, 46, 47, 64, 74, 82, 85, 96, 117
Brown, Jim, 26
Burton, Jeff, 150
Charlotte Motor Speedway, 33, 34, 59
Childress, Richard, 81, 151
Clark, Jeff, 106
Copper Classic, 63
Darlington International Raceway, 32, 37, 39, 48, 61, 63, 82, 95, 113, 126, 131–133, 136, 147
Daytona 500, 49, 52
Daytona International Speedway, 22, 23, 40, 64, 76, 83, 86, 101
Digard Racing Company, 38, 42, 45, 47, 151
Donlavey, Junie, 85, 103
Dover Downs International Speedway, 50, 129, 151
Earnhardt, Dale Sr., 69, 81, 87, 93, 98,106, 115, 145, 149

Lorenzen, Fred, 27, 28
Lowe's Motor Speedway, 18, 35
Lundy, J.T., 52, 79
Maggiacomo, Jocko, 55
Marlin, Clifton "Coo Coo", 103
Marlin, Sterling, 109
Martin, Mark, 74–76, 93, 95, 128, 136, 137, 147
Martinsville Speedway, 61, 65, 83, 86, 89, 150
McClure, Larry, 82, 83, 86
McReynolds, Larry, 45, 48, 60–62, 64–67, 69, 71, 73, 75–77, 82, 87, 92, 97, 100, 114
McReynolds, Robert, 67
McSwaim, Michael, 149
Michigan Speedway, 30, 73, 87, 95, 113, 132
Moody, Ralph, 27–29
Morgan-McClure, 136
Morton, Reed, 95
Nall, Park, 41
NASCAR Winston Cup Illustrated, 92, 94
Nemechek, Joe, 150
Newman, Ducky, 38
North Carolina Speedway, 110
North Wilkesboro Speedway, 34, 71, 88, 93, 97
Orr, Rodney, 86
Owens, Cotton, 32
Parrott, Buddy, 38, 131
Parrott, Debbie, 134
Parrott, Robert, 132
Parrott, Todd, 124, 129, 131–133, 139
Parsons, Benny, 45
Pearson, David, 145
Penske Racing, 131
Petty, Kyle, 66, 76
Petty, Lee, 52,134
Petty, Richard, 30, 52,134, 145
Pocono International Raceway, 45, 54, 72, 73, 76, 79, 107, 109, 132, 138, 140, 148
Ranier, Harry, 48, 52, 56, 79,131
Ranier-Lundy Racing, 48–50, 52, 55
Raymond Beadle Raceway, 46
Richert, Doug, 109

Elder, Jake, 61
Ellington, Hoss, 113
Elliot, Bill, 49, 66, 71–73, 76, 94
Evernham, Ray, 148
Farmer, Red, 63
Fox, Raymond, 87, 107
Foyt, A.J., 49
France, Bill Sr., 22, 73, 78, 141
Gant, Harry, 76
Gant, Libby, 73
Gardner, Bill, 38, 42, 55
Gardner, Jim, 38
Glotzbach, Charlie, 33–35
Gordon, Jeff, 103
Gordon, Robbie, 82
Harper, James, 38
Heidelberg Speedway, 52
Hendrick Motorsports, 45, 58
Hendrick, Rick, 45, 103,147–149
Hickory Motor Speedway, 113
Hmeil, Steve, 86
Holman, John, 27–29
Holman-Moody, 25, 26, 28, 29, 34–36
Howard, Richard, 33, 34, 39
Humphrey, Danielle, 134
Indianapolis Motor Speedway, 120, 132
Irvan, Ernie, 64, 75, 81–83, 85–90, 92, 93–101, 104, 105, 107–111, 114,116, 117, 122, 123, 127, 129,
Irwin, Kenny Jr., 103, 124
Isaac, Bobby, 32
Jarrett, Dale, 89, 100, 103, 105,106,113–116, 117, 119, 120–128, 131, 133–141, 147, 152
Jarret, Ned, 127
Jarrett, Kelley, 119, 120, 134, 137,141
Jarrett, Zachary, 137, 138
Jarrett, Zachary, 137, 138
Johnson, Junior, 23, 32, 34, 37, 39, 47, 64,
Kernan, John, 96
Knuckles, Joey, 48, 64
Kraskopf, Nord, 32
Kulwicki, Alan, 50, 75, 76
Labonte, Terry, 108
Lapage, Kevin, 138

Richmond International Speedway, 76, 85, 111
Rockingham Raceway, 60, 76, 86, 93, 124, 144, 146, 152
Roush Racing, 93
Roush, Jack, 103
Rudd, Ricky, 42, 58,124,143–146, 148–151, 154
Ryan, Terry, 49
Sabates, Felix, 103
Sacks, Greg, 45
Shepherd, Morgan, 62
Smith, Horace "Smitty", 37
Speed, Lake, 82
Stavola Brothers Racing, 42, 55
Stewart, Tony, 103
Sullivan, Jacky "Sully" Sullivan, 28
Talladega Superspeedway, 47, 50, 53, 63, 66, 77, 78, 82, 90, 92, 95,115, 123, 127, 133, 148
Team SABCO, 109
Texas Motor Speedway, 106
Ulrich, D.K., 85
VanDerCook, Brian, 75
Wallace, Kenny, 87, 89
Wallace, Rusty, 46, 131
Waltrip, Darrell, 41, 52, 72, 73, 75
Watkins Glen, 100, 107
Western Carolina Tractor Company, 25, 26, 28
Wilson, Waddell, 45
Wood Brothers, 62,113, 152
Yarborough, Cale, 32, 37, 45, 48,113, 118
Yates, Carolyn, 26, 55, 56,119, 136, 153,
Yates, Doug, 37–39, 94,124,132,138,143, 152, 153,
Yates, Reverend John Clyde, 12, 21
Yates, V.C. Cooke, 12, 21
Yates, Whitney, 138
Yunick, Smokey, 42
Zervakis, Emanuel, 113

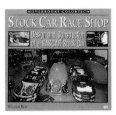

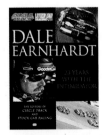